CULTIVATE
SACRED SOIL

Copyright © 2025 by Josh Weisbrod

Published by Arrows and Stones

All rights reserved. No portion of this book may be reproduced, stored in a retrieval system, or transmitted in any form or by any means—electronic, mechanical, photocopy, recording, scanning, or other—except for brief quotations in critical reviews or articles, without prior written permission of the author.

Unless otherwise specified, all Scripture quotations are taken from The ESV® Bible (The Holy Bible, English Standard Version®), copyright © 2001 by Crossway, a publishing ministry of Good News Publishers. Used by permission. All rights reserved. | Scripture quotations marked NIV are taken from the Holy Bible, New International Version®, NIV®. Copyright © 1973, 1978, 1984, 2011 by Biblica, Inc.™ Used by permission of Zondervan. All rights reserved worldwide. www.zondervan.com. The "NIV" and "New International Version" are trademarks registered in the United States Patent and Trademark Office by Biblica, Inc.™

For foreign and subsidiary rights, contact the author.

Cover design by Josh Weisbrod

ISBN: 978-1-964794-20-4   1 2 3 4 5 6 7 8 9 10

Printed in the United States of America

CULTIVATE SACRED SOIL

*Nurture the soil of your heart for
a life that thrives in Christ*

JOSHUA WEISBROD

ARROWS & STONES

To my wife, Katie, whose love and patience brought these pages to life. Thank you for believing in the vision and in me.

CONTENTS

Acknowledgments x
Introduction xii

CHAPTER 1. Changing the Metaphor 18

PART I. CULTIVATE PRESENCE 33
CHAPTER 2. The Life God Created You For 34
CHAPTER 3. Start Digging..................... 48

PART II. CULTIVATE REST 61
CHAPTER 4. True Rest......................... 62
CHAPTER 5. Follow the Leader 72

PART III. CULTIVATE AWE 91
CHAPTER 6. Awesome Splendor 92
CHAPTER 7. Lift Your Eyes 106

PART IV. CULTIVATE PRAYER 121
CHAPTER 8. The Restoration of Prayer 122
CHAPTER 9. From Overgrown to Open 140

PART V. CULTIVATE COMMUNITY 157
CHAPTER 10. Community Increases Growth 158
CHAPTER 11. The Wonderful, Messy
            Work of People.................. 176

PART VI. A CULTIVATED LIFE 193
CHAPTER 12. Get Your Hands Dirty............ 194

ACKNOWLEDGMENTS

The beautiful thing about a healthy church community is that all my friends and family have been actively living out the principles of this book together for years. This writing was made possible because of the loving relationships of so many friends, family members, and fellow ministers of Christ. I could fill another book listing all you have done to make this project possible. I am also grateful to my mother, Sheila Weisbrod, for offering me wise counsel in the areas of spiritual formation. Thank you as well to Dr. Carolyn Tennant for providing direction with my draft and encouraging me to reach for great things. Thanks also to Chris Sonksen for guiding me on how to get this book from my mind to the hands of others, Di Beals for supporting the project so early on, and the many pastors who have helped with reading, editing, or listening. Most importantly, I want to thank my wife Katie, who has heard every word of every chapter a thousand times, and yet each time cheers me on. This book is the product of your patient love amidst late-night writing sessions and garden dirt tracked across the kitchen floor. I promise to sweep up the dirt.

INTRODUCTION

LONGING FOR MORE

I vividly remember the clear, crisp November day when my wife and I drove our first baby home. The reality of what was happening did not hit me until we pulled out of the hospital parking lot. As a new parent, I was driving more cautiously than I had ever driven in my life—ten and two on the steering wheel and five miles under the limit. The only lapse of focus I would allow was a quick glance into the rear-view mirror, hoping to catch a small glimpse of my daughter's red-cheeked face. Suddenly, I was totally overwhelmed with this one thought: *What do we do with this thing?*

In the two days leading up to her birth, I had felt every emotion between joy and fear, but at this moment, I was absolutely struck by the overwhelming reality that this baby was in our care. Here she was, sleeping in our car as we sheepishly drove away as if we had just quietly robbed a bank. I thought that these doctors must have been crazy to allow the care of such a precious child to fall into the hands of the likes of us. This little girl was one of the most beautiful things I had ever seen, and I was completely overwhelmed by the reality of her life. I looked at my wife and said, "What do we do now?"

"WHAT DO I DO NOW?"

You may not have experienced this moment as a parent, but I know many believers who have had a similar reaction when they received new life in Christ. One of the most powerful moments in any person's life is when they profess Jesus Christ as their Lord and Savior. Saying "yes" to Jesus changes everything in our lives.

As Paul says in 2 Corinthians 5:17 (NIV), "The old has gone, the new is here!"

We can feel a myriad of emotions when we sit and dwell on the reality of the new life in Christ we have received. Like a newborn life, it can feel both beautiful and overwhelming at the same time. It is profoundly exciting and wonderful to know the love of Jesus, and at the same time, everything is new and different. We have left an old way of life to step into something completely new. This new life is full of possibility and hope. When we walk with Jesus, we leave behind the path that leads to death and walk an amazing journey of sanctification, purpose, and supernatural power.

I remember attending church and hearing sermon after sermon about how incredible this new life is, how each believer is anointed, and how each of us is called to fulfill the Great Commission. I first have to say this: that idea is very exciting to me. I am overjoyed at the glory and freedom of a life in Christ and the blessing of fulfilling the Great Commission. There is nothing greater to me than the blessing of an intimate relationship with Jesus Christ and the joy of living out the incredible commission of reaching the world with the gospel.

Yet, at the same time, there is another side to that coin. If I am being honest, there were times, like with my newborn daughter, that I was overwhelmed by this new life in Christ. When I began following Jesus, I didn't want a surface-level relationship with Him. I wanted a deep and profound faith. Jesus had changed my entire life; why would I not want to know Him fully and experience all He had to offer? Looking at my faith as if it were a child in my hands, I asked the question: "What do I do with this thing?" Why would God entrust something so great to someone who has no idea what they are doing? Where do I begin? Am I even doing this right?

If you are reading this, you may share some of these thoughts. I have met with countless followers of Christ who have received new life but are unsure of where to go next. I picture it this way: most believers have been handed a newborn life—their new life in Christ—but not given much help on how to grow it. This is an unsettling reality to new believers, but it can even be discouraging for those who have followed Christ for a long time but question why they do not have a deeper, more abundant faith. You might be holding that new life in your hands, asking, "What do I do with this thing?"

If you are longing for more than a surface-level faith, are desperate to know how to live this life with Christ to the fullest, or even feel overwhelmed by what to do next as you begin following Jesus, then you have come to the right place. The answer begins with a simple idea: cultivating your faith.

CULTIVATING FAITH

I believe there is a simple way to deepen your faith. It takes time and effort, but it isn't very complicated. In fact, I can condense it down to one word: cultivation. That one word simply means the tender care needed to bring about abundant life. As we walk through this book, we will unlock different aspects of cultivation that directly deepen our faith. There are multiple facets and practices in our lives that can lead to a deeper faith. The more we walk them out, the more profound and rich our faith will become. This isn't a gardening book, but we will use principles and ideas of agricultural cultivation and the natural world to bring greater visual clarity to the deeper spiritual principles.

FIELDS AND ROADS

Cultivation isn't complicated, but it is multi-faceted. Think of the journey of deepening your faith as if you were looking out over a great farm. Picture yourself standing on a hill and looking out over multiple rolling fields of crops. Some are tilled-up dirt that is ready to be planted; others are covered in small shoots just breaking forth from the ground with great promise, while other fields are full of life and ready to be harvested. Each of these fields represents an area of your faith that can be cultivated for a greater and deeper spiritual harvest. This farm is a place of cultivation known as your new life in Jesus Christ.

As you look out over this place of cultivation, the first field you will see is called Presence. This field is where you will learn how God created you, and how to embrace a greater nearness to Him and awareness of Him in your life.

Scanning the horizon, let your eyes fall on the second field called Rest. In modern culture, this is often the most desired but often extremely neglected field. You may need to do some weeding here but trust me, it will bless your life. In this field, you will discover a beautiful gift from God and work to restore it in your life in a way you have never experienced before.

The third field is a bit further back on your farm, and if you look carefully, you can see it touching the edge of the forest. This is one of the most beautiful fields on the farm, and it is called Awe. By cultivating this field of faith, you will discover the awesome splendor of your Creator revealed through His creation, and allow the awe of God to inform your spiritual growth.

The fourth field is the most significant: Prayer. This field feeds the whole farm, just as restoring prayer as a discipline in your life will feed your soul and deepen your faith in a more profound way.

These separate places of cultivation are wonderful on their own, but they are all linked by another facet of cultivation called Community. The fifth place of cultivation isn't a field at all; it is the roads and rivers that wind through each field, connecting and nourishing them as needed. It is in this final place of cultivation that you will discover the essential role that community has in deepening your Christian faith. Don't skip this one. If you want to truly deepen your faith and move beyond a surface-level walk with Jesus, then community has to be cultivated into a foundational piece of your life.

Each of these areas of cultivation carefully works together to deepen your faith in Christ. As you walk through each field in this book, you will be guided with practical steps to make that specific area flourish to its highest potential. When all these fields are cultivated well, you will see a profound faith well up in your life.

DIG IN!

If you are ready for a deeper faith than you have ever experienced, or if you simply want to understand the beauty of the new life you have received, then it begins right here by cultivating faith. Each of these areas will work together to guide you to a more profound life with Jesus Christ. Invite the Holy Spirit to lead you as you lean into this process of spiritual growth.

CHAPTER 1

CHANGING THE METAPHOR

When people think of Arizona, they mostly think of the greater Phoenix area with its rocks, cacti, scorpions, and heat. If that's what you pictured, then you would be right. Though parts of this state have lush pine forests, the valley is a desert full of all the crawling bugs and spikey plants you could imagine. I have seen a bobcat fight a rattlesnake in the middle of a cul-de-sac, my family owns a desert tortoise that burrows ten feet underground, and I have cooked an egg on the tailgate of my truck—all classic Arizona style.

You might be surprised to hear then that when I moved my family here in 2016, I dove deep into gardening. Why would someone move from Washington to Phoenix and become a gardener? Isn't gardening in Arizona just playing in the sand? Now, I could give you a list of reasons why the valley is suitable for growing and fifteen book references about water conservation in arid gardening. Still, the actual reason I started gardening is that I like growing things. The time-consuming, dirty art of growing plants is inspiring to me.

People usually have two widely varying reactions to the topic of gardening. Some are very curious and joyfully receptive to the topic, while others are filled with anxiety even thinking about how to raise a plant. Whether you have a green thumb, or your mere gaze could kill a zucchini plant, everyone can learn one fundamental principle from gardening: **cultivation**. This principle changed the way I approached life. In fact, the simple principle of cultivation revolutionized the way I approached faith in Jesus Christ. It gave me a new way of deepening my faith in Christ. If you want a deeper, more profound life in Jesus, then cultivation is the answer. Let's unpack this term a little bit as we prepare to apply it to our faith.

AGRICULTURE, CULTIVATION, AND FAITH

From an agricultural perspective, *cultivation is preparing and using the ground to grow something*. When farmers till and plant their vast fields they are actively participating in the work of cultivation. When a gardener plants a small box of vegetables, they are also cultivating.

When we moved to Arizona, I dove head-on into the passion of gardening. My wife and I bought a small house near Arizona State University, and it became my cultivation classroom for six years. Our little backyard in Tempe was hardly an epicenter of agricultural opportunity, but the small plot of land taught me so much about the principle of cultivation. I had volunteered at full-scale farms in the past, but this small yard in the valley of the sun transformed my thinking.

Slowly, I planted trees, constructed garden beds, and learned every possible way to kill a tomato plant. If you didn't know, there are many ways to kill a tomato plant, and I learned them all. Over the next six years, I realized that cultivation is more than digging in the dirt and hoping for a harvest. **Cultivation is the work of tender care necessary to bring great things out of even the most minuscule life.** While gardening in the Arizona heat, I learned what to nurture, prune, and get rid of. The discovery was slow but deeply informative.

Working in the dirt over and over will make you keenly aware of humanity's place in creation. Suddenly, seasons become more than changes in clothing options; they teach you about the changes in life and the need for patience. When you cultivate the earth, winter is a time of expectation, spring is about new life, summer is about endurance, and fall is about abundance. If you are willing to look and listen, every part of the cultivation teaches something. Seeds teach that you cannot force growth; you must only patiently steward and nurture it. The sun, wind, and rain teach you how small you are in the universe. You can learn endless spiritual principles in gardening, and many of them can translate to help you better grasp your life in Christ.

This is why Jesus uses many agricultural examples when teaching His disciples and followers. It isn't because He was speaking to a solely agrarian society and needed a simple metaphor they could understand. After all, if audience contextualization were the goal, then Christ would have used more marketplace examples. Jesus used these agricultural examples because the work of cultivation is present in all His creations, including our lives. Nature, stewardship, and cultivation principles are woven into our created being. They even inform the way we understand Jesus Christ. He is the Good Shepherd, the Wise Gardener, the Seed that must die to bring life. These are cultivating ideas used to teach the deep things of faith.

> CULTIVATION IS NOT SIMPLY ABOUT WHAT WE DO BUT HOW WE DO IT.

Each agricultural cultivation example Christ gives in Scripture was part of His more incredible teaching about the kingdom of God and how we, as disciples, were called to live. In the same way, this book features the principles of cultivation to help deepen our faith in Christ. Every example from the garden or nature is meant to point us toward principles and practices that will open up a more profound intimacy with God and transform how we live our lives. Cultivation is not simply about what we do but how we do it. It is about how we live.

A BROKEN METAPHOR

Down the hill from my old house in rainy western Washington stands a massive lumberyard. Its large steel structure casts a robust and shapely presence against the backdrop of the snow-tipped Cascade Mountains. Every day, the steam would rise up from the factory and dissipate into the damp clouds regularly hanging around the bend of our little town. The main road to the next town wove directly in front of the lumberyard, and if you were paying attention, you could catch a glimpse of a large wooden sign stamped with the words "Days since last accident." Underneath those words was a fading black chalkboard, long worn from the aggressive wiping of jacket sleeves, bearing the number forty-three. Every time a worker made a mistake that was classified as an accident, the board would have to be wiped clean. I drove by that sign often, and sometimes, it would read one hundred, and other days it would shamefully display a one or two. The idea in the lumberyard is that every worker must do everything in their power to not reset that number to zero. That is the definition of success in that environment.

This simple visual is highly representative of how many Christians view their faith. They long for the deeper things of Christ but feel like they are always starting over. They have been taught that their new life in Christ is in a constant state of reset. In their minds, repentance is a tragedy by which they are thrust back onto day zero. They work day in and day out to make sure they never have to make the walk of shame to the blackboard, wipe out their success number, and draw a big zero on the board. For this reason, many believers who long for greater spiritual maturity end up in the same old cycles of behavior over and over. To them, following Christ is about simply avoiding mistakes rather than growing in holiness. This is not an advocation for purposefully disobeying God but a recognition that our way of thinking must change to allow for better growth. The understanding and systems by which many people have oriented their faith are broken, and they will not lead them into more profound intimacy with God. There is a better metaphor, a more vibrant way to understand our faith in Christ. If we begin to shift our thinking, we will see that there is a more profound life in Jesus, which He longs for us to have.

A NEW LIFE

Spiritual maturity is about growth. It is far more beautiful and complex than a light switch we turn on or off. It is a journey of sanctification. So, if we want to live out this journey of growth, we need to define it with growth-based terminology. The pass/fail mindset might help us stay scared and potentially obedient, but it lacks the guidance to open our hearts to the abundance of our new life in Christ. Do you realize that your life as a believer is entirely new?

One of the most powerful moments in any person's life is when they profess Jesus Christ as their Lord and Savior. He doesn't become merely an addition to our lives; He becomes our lives. This is why Paul passionately writes to the Galatians that he has been born again into Christ, and the life he now leads is by the resurrection of Christ: "I have been crucified with Christ. It is no longer I who live, but Christ who lives in me. And the life I now live in the flesh I live by faith in the Son of God, who loved me and gave himself for me" (Galatians 2:20).

Paul professes something compelling here: following Christ means living in His resurrection. When we repent of our sins and believe in the risen Christ, our old life is dead, and our new life in Him begins. Salvation is a total life exchange of a dead sinful life for an eternal resurrection life. This means salvation in Jesus Christ is not an upgrade to your life; He is your life. Jesus rose from the dead on the third day to bring you into the fullness of His resurrection life today and for eternity. Salvation is not simply life-affecting; it is life-changing. This new life in Christ is a source of immense joy and hope.

When I was younger, I remember often hearing the term "born again" used to describe someone who had given their life to Christ. This small phrase is vital to understanding our life in Christ. One day, Jesus encounters a curious man named Nicodemus, who has big questions about how to enter the kingdom of God. Jesus tells Nicodemus, "Truly, truly, I say to you, unless one is born again, he cannot see the kingdom of God" (John 3:3). Nicodemus is confused about what kind of birth Jesus is referring to because he is thinking solely of physical birth. Jesus, on the other hand, is referring to a birth by the Spirit. Salvation is being born again by the Spirit of God.

> *Jesus answered, "Truly, truly, I say to you, unless one is born of water and the Spirit, he cannot enter the kingdom of God. That which is born of the flesh is flesh, and that which is born of the Spirit is spirit. Do not marvel that I said to you, 'You must be born again.' The wind blows where it wishes, and you hear its sound, but you do not know where it comes from or where it goes. So it is with everyone who is born of the Spirit."* —John 3:5-8

Everyone enters this new life in Christ as a spiritual infant. No one begins their faith as a fully formed, spiritually mature individual. Every single believer must grow up in the faith just as every human is born as an infant and must grow to physical maturity. Notice the vital term: grow. Spiritual maturity has always been about growth. Being a disciple of Christ is a journey on which we spend time with Him and learn from Him, how to live like Him. Tapping into a deep and rich faith begins by growing to be like Christ day by day, moment by moment. It is a careful, nurturing process and rarely an explosive moment. I have never met someone who became a fully mature believer in a flash of light. For most people, the road to spiritual maturity was paved by their patient and diligent care of their new life in Christ.

A NEW METAPHOR

It was the act of gardening that first reshaped the way I understood the journey of spiritual maturity. I, myself, had fallen victim to a broken way of thinking about my new life in Christ, but gardening changed my whole mindset. If you want a more profound relationship with Christ, it comes through cultivating your faith. Let's dive in and expand this metaphor for a minute.

> **THE WORD OF GOD IS PERFECT, BUT OUR HEARTS MUST BE THE KIND OF SOIL THAT WELCOMES THE WORD OF CHRIST.**

Think about discipleship like cultivating a garden with Christ. Picture a small rectangular garden bed, full of dirt but vacant of plant life. That barren dirt is the very beginning of each of our lives. When Jesus teaches about the work of the gospel, He shares that it is like a sower who casts seeds on the ground. Jesus says that the seed lands on a variety of different soils. Some of the seed finds hard ground where it is trampled and stolen by the enemy, some lands on the rocky ground and is torn out by the winds of trouble and worry, and some finds root, but their fruit is choked out by weeds of sinful passions. The prosperous seed lands on good soil, where it takes root and brings about an abundant harvest. The quality of the gospel remains the same in every setting, but the condition of the soil determines if it is received, finds root, and brings a harvest. In the same way, your heart is the soil. Your reception to the gospel was dependent on the condition of the soil, and that continues to be true. The Word of God is perfect, but our hearts must be the kind of soil that welcomes the word of Christ.

If you are living in the new life of Jesus, then your garden is not barren dirt anymore; it is a resting place of life. Picture the life of a new believer as a garden bed with the very first sprigs of each plant breaking through the soil. Some will grow faster, while others may take longer, just as each of us will easily flourish in some areas of the faith while wrestling in others. No one blames each plant for maturing at different times, and in the same way, you should find peace knowing different spiritual disciplines in your life will mature in their proper time.

As each of those plants begins growing toward the sun, it is the gardener's job to cultivate that garden. This means the gardener must spend intentional time and give diligent care to nurture every part of the garden bed. Cultivation is how the garden bed will bring forth a great harvest. Picture for a second that you are kneeling next to the garden, which represents your life, and right next to you is the Master Gardener, Jesus Christ. If you were next to a master gardener in a physical garden, you would ask him to show you what to prune, what to fertilize, what to be patient with, and what to weed out. In the same way, we ask Christ to reveal to us by the Spirit the places in our journey which need care. In every life, in varying seasons, there are parts of our faith that must be left alone, weeded out, pruned, or harvested.

The goal of all this cultivation is to grow and harvest the garden. As you grow in faith, the act of cultivation will come naturally. What was once difficult will be easy. The weeds of sin will become easier to spot and remove. You will become increasingly patient with harvest schedules and even become in tune with the rhythm of each spiritual season. It is about learning to nurture, protect, and cultivate the seeds of God's love and grace in our hearts so that they may bear fruit and bring life to the world around us. Just as a gardener tends to their garden with patience and dedication, we are called to cultivate our relationship with God, allowing His transformative power to work in us and through us.

ABIDE IN THE VINE

"I am the true vine, and my Father is the vinedresser. Every branch in me that does not bear fruit he takes away, and every branch that does bear fruit he prunes, that it may bear more fruit. Already you are clean because of the word that I have spoken to you. Abide in me, and I in you. As the branch cannot bear fruit by itself, unless it abides in the vine, neither can you, unless you abide in me. I am the vine; you are the branches. Whoever abides in me and I in him, he it is that bears much fruit, for apart from me you can do nothing." —John 15:1-5

When Jesus teaches His disciples to be united with Him and bear great fruit, He implores them to abide in Him. Jesus is the true vine, and He invites His disciples to experience the tender care of the Master Gardener, who efficiently prunes away the dead and brings forth fruit from every life. I had always thought the imagery of the Lord tending a vineyard was very poetic, but I began to understand the teaching more deeply when I planted grapevines two years ago.

Grapevines have an incredible capacity for growth. They can grow almost ten feet long in a single season, and the central vine puts out dozens of main shoots in every direction imaginable.

If this visual sounds messy, it's because it is. I let the grapevines run wild during the first year of planting, assuming that this wild cultivation would bring the best harvest. I was wrong. Not every branch produces fruit. I learned quickly that too many branches growing without careful pruning will block the fruiting branches from receiving enough light to produce fully developed grapes. Gardeners and vinedressers must prune the non-fruiting nodes away so that the fruiting branches can have room and light to grow.

This year, I decided to do a test with two similar grapevines planted side by side. Having read a few books on vine pruning, I heavily pruned one vine while barely touching the other. When the growing season came, the unpruned vine looked spectacular and green, but the differences became evident as the season went on. The unpruned vine was wild but faded quickly while putting out little fruit. The heavily pruned vine started smaller, but eventually, it filled out and was covered in fragrant grape clusters. Pruning enabled the vine to reach its full potential and brought about a greater harvest.

A good gardener prunes a plant because he loves it and wants to see it bring about great fruit. That is the essence of cultivation. That is the journey Christ is inviting all of us on. He is the careful Gardener who invites us into the work of cultivating our faith so that it can be fruitful. He longs for us to reach the full potential of our faith. Jesus wants His followers to experience deep intimacy with Him, build His church, see the miraculous works of the Spirit, and engage in all the kingdom has to offer today and for eternity. Cultivating a life with Christ means nurturing the soil of the heart to prepare a place for this deeper communion with him. Cultivating areas of our spiritual life prepare a place for the fruit of the Holy Spirit to burst forth.

As I sat in my simple garden, reflecting on the work of the Gardener (Father God), I opened up the Word of God and prayerfully asked for guidance from the Holy Spirit. In this peaceful place, I asked the Holy Spirit to reveal areas in my life that need cultivating. The Holy Spirit began to work in my life that day, and over the next few years, I more deeply understood how I could cultivate a healthy relationship with Christ. Even today, I am still learning to nurture my faith in Christ, but every day is an opportunity to grow a little more in each area. If you want to deepen your faith in Jesus Christ, it starts small and grows. Tremendous growth can come by cultivating a few different areas of your spiritual life: presence, rest, awe, prayer, and community. Each area is cultivated differently, but all require careful nurturing to produce a harvest of deep faith. This book will explore why each cultivation area is essential for a fulfilling life and how each area can be developed.

GET MESSY

Gardening is messy work, but the harvest is worth it! Every gardener I've met has had dirt on their fingers and scratches on their hands; they're like a badge of honor, a sign of nurturing life. Over time, I have learned that anyone charged with cultivating life carries the dirt and marks of that work. Parents understand this principle very quickly. I don't know any parent whose car, home, or body doesn't show visible signs of raising a child. Their life has become a testament to the reality of cultivating a precious gift.

As we delve into the various aspects of spiritual growth and development, it's important to remember that the journey may not always be smooth or easy. We may encounter messy moments and face challenges that seem overwhelming. These experiences may stretch and push us in new and unexpected ways. However, keep going despite these obstacles. Approach them with patience and a nurturing spirit, just as we would with a tender garden. By embracing the process of cultivating our lives with Christ, we open ourselves up to the promise of His presence, enriching every aspect of our lives. Embracing the mess and staying committed to the journey will ultimately lead to a deep and fulfilling spiritual connection with Christ.

CULTIVATE PRESENCE

CHAPTER 2

THE LIFE GOD CREATED YOU FOR

The weather forecast says that today's temperatures will break one hundred degrees. That might sound like a death sentence for some people, but we call it spring around here. The morning is warming up, and the day's activities are beginning. White-tail doves land randomly on the dirt, searching for remnants of seed or the occasional ill-fated bug. Meanwhile, our backyard chickens are hopping out of their coop to retake their territory from the invading birds while ensuring their presence is heard around the neighborhood. The air is warm, but the occasional breeze moves through the leaves of the trees and sounds like cool water rushing by. I know it's not cold, but something about it reminds me of a stream and brings me peace.

When we bought this house, the whole backyard was turf and concrete. You couldn't count a single plant in the entire yard. It would get hot, boiling hot. By mid-day in the summer, the heat from the ground alone would have me contemplating what an eternity in hell must feel like. But I have worked hard over the past few years to relieve our yard from the oppressive heat. I planted trees, vines, bushes, and anything else to bring the yard to life. I spent many days moving rock, digging holes, planting seeds or saplings, carefully pruning branches, and praying for the best—cultivation in motion.

Beneath the sprawling canopy of the twenty-five-foot moringa tree, I find solace for my morning thoughts. Not long ago, a tiny seed birthed this majestic tree. A steaming cup of Seattle's rich coffee cradled in my hands is an indelible link to my cherished heritage. As daybreak unfolds, our modest backyard teems with life, each sight and sound a symphony of awakening. Yet amidst the rustling leaves and the warbling birds, it is the melodic laughter of my children that truly stirs my soul.

In the early light of morning, my youngest takes his first wobbly steps to the garden, eager to pluck not-quite-ripe cherry tomatoes from a lush bush that could hide a Volkswagen bug. The joy in my children's eyes as they roam the garden isn't just about harvesting flat peas or uprooting premature carrots. It's a deeper love, rooted in a greater love and blossoming with each new day.

In my absence, the garden lies still, untouched by tiny hands. My children do not roam among the bushes plucking fruit; it is as if my presence is the invisible thread that draws them there. Their desire is to be with me, and this realization nearly moves me to tears. It's not the abundance of fruit they cherish but the shared moments with me in the garden. The flat peas are delightful, yet it's the act of strolling and conversing with me that they hold dear amidst the garden's embrace. Sometimes, we talk about life, and I listen to them explain the good and bad of all that is happening in their world, and sometimes, they are content with me simply being present. Sometimes we work on a task as menial and gross as disposing of chicken poop into the composter, and yet they don't seem to mind. The garden has become a place of presence with my children. They enjoy being with their father.

As I reflect on the moments spent in the garden with my children, I am awestruck by the immense value of a father's presence in a child's life. I've discovered that a father's presence is among the most profound gifts he can bestow upon his children. This revelation has profoundly shaped my perception of my bond with my heavenly Father. I yearn to bask in the presence of my heavenly

Father, just as my children find joy in our time together in the garden. This innate need for closeness is divinely ingrained within us. We are fashioned to thrive in communion and intimacy with our heavenly Father. This profound realization has reshaped my understanding of the significance of cultivating a sense of presence in our human connections and spiritual journey with God.

CREATED FOR PRESENCE

God created you and me to live in His presence. In the beginning, God created man and placed him in the garden of Eden.

Man was not separate from creation; he was part of it. Our connection with the Creator is different than all the rest of creation because we were uniquely made in God's image to live in a relationship with Him. He created many good things—oceans, mountains, animals, plants—but He made humanity in His image.

God placed the first man, Adam, in the garden of Eden to live in communion with Him. This relationship between man and God meant that Adam lived in the absolute purest sense of the presence of God. Just imagine a stunning and breathtaking garden overflowing with the glorious presence of the Almighty God. Envision yourself relaxing in this perfect garden when, suddenly, the entire presence of God strolls through. It's an incredible scene to picture. According to Scripture, God used to walk in the garden and communicate with humanity. In the beginning, Adam cherished moments spent in the garden with his heavenly Father, much like how my children enjoy time with me in our little backyard garden. Similarly, as a child of God, Adam experienced the blessing and felt the full benefit of his Father's presence in the garden.

> *Then the LORD God formed the man of dust from the ground and breathed into his nostrils the breath of life, and the man became a living creature. And the Lord God planted a garden in Eden, in the east, and there he put the man whom he had formed.* —Genesis 2:7-8

This first relationship between Adam and God symbolized the profound significance of living in communion with the Creator, highlighting the inherent desire for closeness with God woven into human existence.

I can't even imagine the joy Adam must have experienced spending that time with the heavenly Father in the perfect garden of Eden. When my kids see me head out to the garden, they light up. My youngest son starts banging on the sliding glass door if we don't let him toddle his way out there. He desires to be in the garden with his father with all his little heart. Adam's experience with God must have eclipsed even the most incredible joy my children could feel in the garden with me. My kids and I love to rest together in the cool shade and work in the dirt in the little garden beds, but the rest and purpose Adam felt in the garden with God was perfect beyond what we could comprehend.

PURPOSE IN THE PRESENCE

The idea of lounging around in a garden and having God drop by like a sitcom neighbor might sound appealing, but the actual relationship between God and man in Eden was far more profound. The garden was a place of both deep rest and purposeful mission. It was a space where Adam and Eve experienced the profound rest of being in the presence of God while also being tasked with the meaningful mission of tending and cultivating the garden. This combination of rest and mission speaks to the richness and complexity of the relationship between humanity and the divine in the garden of Eden.

The garden of Eden exemplifies pure rest due to man's relationship with and access to God's presence. The Lord is the truest source of rest, so to commune with Him is to be in a physical and spiritual state of rest. The garden was a place without sin and with complete communion with God, so Adam and Eve's souls could rest completely.

> GOD CREATED EVERY PERSON ON PURPOSE FOR A PURPOSE.

Man didn't sit around in the garden eating fruit and becoming lazy. God gave man a purpose in the garden, which He called work. Though in contrast to the frenzied tempo of our contemporary world, the garden might have appeared as a realm of comparative stillness, it marked the dawn of humanity's purpose. When the Lord positioned Adam in the garden, it was not for idle waiting or chance encounters; it was for a purpose bestowed by the Divine.

God created every person on purpose for a purpose. He imbued your life with a sense of purpose. God created humanity in His image from the very first day. Genesis tells us that when God placed Adam in Eden, He already had a purpose for him: "The Lord God took the man and put him in the garden of Eden to work it and keep it" (Genesis 2:15). God charged Adam to put his energy and effort into the garden by working it and commissioned him to maintain it through good stewardship or "keeping" it. Cultivation involves the physical effort of working the ground and stewarding it well. God gave man the purpose of cultivating a place for His presence at the beginning of creation. That is an incredible purpose: to live in communion with God and cultivate a place where the presence of God will dwell.

FROM PRESENCE TO PAIN

Unfortunately, sin destroyed this beautiful expression of communion with God when it came into the world. When God gave Adam purpose, He also gave him instructions on how to live out this purpose, but Adam and Eve rebelled against God's commands and instead gave into Satan's deception. The choice to eat of the tree of the knowledge of good and evil introduced sin into the world and changed everything.

God had given Adam the task of cultivating a place for the presence of the Lord. However, Adam stained that place with sin against God. When I talk about the place of communion with God, I'm not just referring to Eden; I'm also referring to Adam's heart. The communion with God didn't just happen because God likes gardens but because God loves His children and desires to have a relationship with them. In a perfect Eden, that union with a perfect God is possible, but when sin entered the world, it destroyed that communion, first for Adam and Eve and then for the rest of humanity.

The destruction of Eden was partially in physical communion in the garden and, more profoundly, spiritual destruction in man's heart. Because of that choice, humanity could no longer live in direct communion with God's presence. Since the curse of sin expelled man from God's presence, they also lost their rest and purpose. This result is stained across the pages of history, a story of humanity without peace and purpose, giving into the rebellion against God. In a fallen world, work became toil, rest became impossible, and the children of God moved from presence to pain:

> *And to Adam he said, "Because you have listened to the voice of your wife and have eaten of the tree of which I commanded you, 'You shall not eat of it,' cursed is the ground because of you; in pain you shall eat of it all the days of your life; thorns and thistles it shall bring forth for you; and you shall eat the plants of the field. By the sweat of your face you shall eat bread, till you return to the ground, for out of it you were taken; for you are dust, and to dust you shall return."* —Genesis 3:17-19

THE WORK OF RESTORATION

The good news is that God has been working to restore communion with His beloved creation from the beginning. His first promise is, "And I will put enmity between you and the woman, and between your offspring and hers; he will crush your head, and you will strike his heel" (Genesis 3:15, NIV). This scripture promises a victory that God will fulfill in the future through the coming Messiah.

As a teacher of the Word of God, I am particularly fascinated by the theme of Jesus Christ throughout the Bible. This motif is often referred to as the scarlet thread, and it signifies how all of Scripture points to the coming Messiah, His death, and His resurrection. Understanding this principle helps us gain a more contextual and precise picture of the Law God gives to his people, Israel. If you've ever tried to read the Bible in a year, you might have found it challenging to get through the Old Testament Books of the Law, such as Genesis, Exodus, Leviticus, Numbers, and Deuteronomy. However, these books are more than just a list of rules for the people of Israel; they are essential scriptures that reveal God's ongoing work of restoration and how the children of Israel could live in communion with Him.

A casual reader of Old Testament Law might wonder how commands for Sabbath observance or detailed tabernacle worship procedures had any meaning for their lives. God spoke these laws for His people, so they would learn to walk in communion with Him as His children and prepare for the Messiah. For example, the law of the Sabbath was more than simply a day of rest. It taught the Jewish people to remember God's perfect rest at creation while giving them a holy desire for when He would bring proper rest to the earth again through Christ. The various sacrifices that the Jewish people offered were a recognition of the blood required to take away their sins and restore them to communion. God spoke and inspired the Old Testament Law and the Prophets to point the children of God to the coming Messiah who would finally restore His creation to their created intent. Even now, the Word points believers to the day in which each person will experience the fullness of rest and restoration to the presence of God:

> *For God was pleased to have all his fullness dwell in him, and through him to reconcile to himself all things, whether things on earth or things in heaven, by making peace through his blood, shed on the cross. —Colossians 1:19-20 (NIV)*

THE RESURRECTION IS RESTORATION

From the very moment sin destroyed the intimacy by which man had access to the presence of God, the Lord was preparing a way to restore His creation. Humanity is restored to life in the presence of God by Jesus Christ. In John 14:6, Jesus doesn't offer that He is "a" way to live in God's presence, but instead that He is "the" way to live eternally in God's presence: "Jesus answered, 'I am the way and the truth and the life. No one comes to the Father except through me'" (John 14:6, NIV). Regardless of how the world markets the accessibility of heaven, the reality is that the only way back to communion with Father God is through His Son, Jesus Christ:

> *And he is the head of the body, the church; he is the beginning and the firstborn from among the dead, so that in everything he might have the supremacy. For God was pleased to have all his fullness dwell in him, and through him to reconcile to himself all things, whether things on earth or things in heaven, by making peace through his blood, shed on the cross. —Colossians 1:18-20 (NIV)*

Sin created a divide where there was intimacy. The resurrection restored that intimacy with God's presence. When Jesus died on the cross for the sins of the world, He tore open the curtain in the holy of holies. For centuries, the curtain had separated the people of God from the most intimate form of His presence dwelling among them. Only the high priest could go into the holy of holies and stand in the presence of God. The high priest had to go through a litany of purification rights for months to prepare to enter God's presence. Only a holy man could go into the most sacred place of the temple. The average person could never experience the depth of presence in the holy of holies. When Jesus took the sins of humanity on the cross, He became the once-and-for-all sacrificial lamb. No longer did Israel need to find a perfect, spotless lamb to sacrifice and pour out the blood for their sins. Jesus was that lamb. He is also our new High Priest:

> *Since then we have a great high priest who has passed through the heavens, Jesus, the Son of God, let us hold fast our confession. For we do not have a high priest who is unable to sympathize with our weaknesses, but one who in every respect has been tempted as we are, yet without sin. Let us then with confidence draw near to the throne of grace, that we may receive mercy and find grace to help in time of need. —Hebrews 4:14-16*

Hebrews is a testament to Jesus as our High Priest. You have access to God's holy presence because of Jesus. What Jesus did on the cross provides every believer with access to God's holy presence, and His eventual return will fully restore this life of presence. His blood restored you, and it is still restoring you, and it will continue to restore you until His second coming at the end of the age.

ARE YOU SURE?

Many people can hear the message that Christ has restored us to a life of presence with God but struggle to believe it daily. Maybe it is because they struggle to have faith in something they cannot control, or perhaps it's a general sense of unworthiness and shame still clinging on even after salvation. Here is the good news: the presence of God is with you today. You have special access to the presence of God because of the Holy Spirit. Before His death, Jesus promises His disciples, "But the Advocate, the Holy Spirit, whom the Father will send in my name, will teach you all things and will remind you of everything I have said to you" John 14:26 (NIV). In the name of Jesus, the Father sends the Spirit to dwell with us. The Holy Spirit assures every believer of their life of presence with God because of the Spirit who is within our innermost being.

> THE PRESENCE OF GOD DOES HAVE A CONDITION: HE WILL NOT FORCE HIS WAY INTO A HOME THAT DOES NOT INVITE HIM.

Trying to cultivate a life of presence without the Holy Spirit would be like trying to grow a garden without water. No matter how big your garden is, it must be saturated with water to support life. I don't care how good the seed is, how ready the soil is, or how bright the sun is; if it is not saturated, it cannot support life. The water must permeate every part and every molecule of the soil, and in the same way, the Spirit must permeate every part of our lives to the deep places of our innermost being. It is in our innermost being where the work of cultivation begins because it is there that the presence of God resides in the Holy Spirit. To begin cultivating a life of presence, you must first invite the Holy Spirit to take residence in your innermost being and follow His leadership.

It's remarkable how many believers spend years trying to work for God but very little time inviting His presence into every part of their lives. It's as if the Spirit has visited them at home, but instead of letting Him dwell, they keep bringing gift after gift to the front porch, hoping to receive His blessing. The truth is that the blessing comes from the Spirit dwelling within the home. The Holy Spirit's presence cultivates an authentic life of abundance. The Holy Spirit longs to commune with you, but you must allow Him in. When I say permission, I'm not suggesting that you need a special code or that you can control the Spirit. However, the presence of God does have a condition: He will not force His way into a home that does not invite Him. To give the Spirit permission is to recognize that a life of abundance begins when He dwells fully in your heart. You must surrender to God and declare to the Spirit that you will obey His leadership in every way. Reflect on this essential question: *Is my life a dwelling place for God's presence?* Take the time to ponder whether you have allowed the Spirit full access to every aspect of your life to cultivate and enrich His presence. This heartfelt introspection can motivate a dedicated and fervent resolve to invite God's presence into every corner of your existence.

CHAPTER 3

START DIGGING

Growing a plant is one thing, but cultivating a garden is an entirely different process. To grow a plant, all you need to do is go to the local nursery or hardware store, buy a pot, some dirt, and a tomato plant, and put them all together. Assuming you remember to water it, you should be all right. Cultivating a garden is a much more complex process.

It is more of a multi-seasonal, hands-on relationship than a simple step-by-step process. To truly cultivate something takes the tedious but satisfying work of using your senses to become keenly aware of the nuance in the garden. Sure, all plants share similar broad-stroke needs—water, soil, nitrogen, sun—but every plant is different and has different individual needs. On top of that, every soil is nuanced as well. Soil is more than just dirt; it must sustain life and provide the environment for plants to grow. A great gardener knows that they are, first and foremost, cultivating soil.

Cultivating a life of presence with God is not a simple task. Often, God's presence is referred to as a drive-thru in the church: swing on in, get what you need, and head on out. However, the kind of presence we need to cultivate is not a fleeting encounter but a continuous, deep, and intimate relationship with God. Like the gardener, each believer must engage in a multi-seasonal effort to cultivate a life that can welcome and grow in the abiding presence of God.

Each field has varying soil, but the seed remains the same. The fundamental truth of Christ is the same for all people, but the nuance of how we respond and interact with His presence is as diverse as the soil. Some soils are rocky, some wetlands, and some complete sand. People have different pasts that inform their understanding, different personalities that change how they approach God, and even wildly varying levels of personal knowledge or experience with the values and ideas of Christ. That means how they must be cultivated and stewarded is different, even though the seeds are all the same.

The work of cultivation has to be personal to the life of each believer, just as each soil must be uniquely tended. Each gardener must focus on preparing a place where the seed can grow, and each believer must practically concentrate on preparing their heart to cultivate a life of presence. This can be done through regular prayer, studying the Scriptures, and participating in worship. Our desire should be to carefully prepare a good place for the presence of God to rule and reign in our lives. This work is learned through time, but it is time worth spending. It's a personal journey of growth and discovery.

IT'S A LIFE WORTH CULTIVATING

This cultivation area is first because it becomes the foundation for every other area we will discuss in this book. If it feels a bit abstract, don't worry. Walking through the different cultivation areas will illuminate your understanding of this area more clearly. For now, what is important to remember is that a life in God's presence is worth cultivating. It's not just a duty; it's a joy. God wants to have a deep relationship with you, and just like Paul wrote, I also hope that you would experience how wide, how long, how high, and how deep God's love is for you (see Ephesians 3:18-20). A life of presence with God is not a burden; it's a blessing. Many ways I approach God's presence changed when I realized it was the most blessed place and posture I could possibly be in. It didn't feel out of place; it felt like I had finally found my purpose. How we approach God will dramatically change when we begin to see His presence as an abundant blessing. When Christ redeemed us through His death and resurrection, He provided a way to live completely in the wonderful presence of God. His presence is a garden full of the abundant fruit of His goodness, and so we should desire to cultivate this area well. Here is how to begin.

WALK BY THE SPIRIT

Before ascending to heaven, Christ promised to send the Holy Spirit. He then fulfilled that promise in Acts 2 by sending tongues of fire to the believers in the upper room. But even though a believer has received the Holy Spirit, internal growth still needs to be done. In fact, upon receiving the Spirit, every believer is simply beginning a more remarkable journey of learning to be led by the Spirit. This journey is not one of solitude but of empowerment and guidance. "Walking by the Spirit" means living in a way that aligns with the Spirit's guidance and direction, allowing the Spirit to lead and influence our thoughts, words, and actions. It is a crucial practice in cultivating a life of presence with God.

In his letter to the Galatian church, Paul urges them to walk by the Spirit so that they will not gratify the desires of the flesh (see Galatians 5:16). Paul understood that there is a struggle within every person between the flesh and the Spirit. He is even honest enough to share his lament of not doing what he wants to do while also doing what he doesn't want to do. The epistles are full of references to the internal war between flesh and Spirit. Even in the pursuit of presence, our flesh will war against us. Yet we are also told that we will be victorious when we submit the flesh to the Spirit:

> *So, I say, walk by the Spirit, and you will not gratify the desires of the flesh. For the flesh desires what is contrary to the Spirit, and the Spirit what is contrary to the flesh. They are in conflict with each other, so that you are not to do whatever you want. But if you are led by the Spirit, you are not under the law. —Galatians 5:16-18 (NIV)*

Let me tell you how I really feel about small groups. At our church, we believe small groups are vital for spiritual formation. They provide a place where believers build one another up in faith toward Christ and provide opportunities for actual spiritual growth. I love leading small groups and providing a place for people to become a family, learn from the Word, and love their neighbors. I will be candid, though: even as the church pastor, there is a moment before some small groups when I genuinely dislike them. Hear me out. I love my small group all week leading up to the meeting time, but the hour before the group, I feel my flesh telling me to cancel. Something in me says, *You could pretend to be sick or just stay home.*

My flesh fights against what my Spirit knows will cultivate a healthy life with Christ. If you have ever battled with your flesh, then you know the feeling I am talking about. Our flesh longs for worldly things, while the Spirit offers the more significant things of God. Our flesh does not want us to pursue the presence of God, yet our spirit knows that a life of presence is a blessing. This is not an easy struggle, but we are called to engage in it. The struggle is that our flesh is powerful, but the blessing is that the Spirit is much greater. When I submit my flesh and engage in what I know is good for my faith, I am reminded of what a blessing it is. I am renewed when I don't let that small voice trick me into missing out on the community I love dearly. Candidly, I genuinely love small groups. I always leave the group so refreshed and overjoyed. Still, it required denying my flesh and submitting to the Spirit to press into what I know will grow my faith. Praise the Lord that when we choose to walk by the Spirit instead of our flesh, it cultivates a place of profound spiritual growth.

If we walk by the flesh, then our life's purpose is wrapped up in the fruit of the flesh. Our life becomes a hedonistic game of Hungry Hungry Hippos, desperately snatching up all the things we want before we die. If we walk according to the Spirit, our lives become a more internally peaceful practice of abiding in the Spirit's presence and seeing Him bring about the fruit. When Paul writes of the fruit of the Spirit, it is not a shopping list of faith. The title "Fruit of the Spirit" encompasses multiple listed fruits. This is because when we cultivate a life of presence, the Spirit's values manifest in our lives. The Spirit and Christ Jesus are revealed through the active work of cultivating a life of presence. You can cultivate a life of presence in three ways: embrace God's Word, pursue holiness, and participate in pure worship.

> *But the fruit of the Spirit is love, joy, peace, forbearance, kindness, goodness, faithfulness, gentleness and self-control. Against such things, there is no law. Those who belong to Christ Jesus have crucified the flesh with its passions and desires. Since we live by the Spirit, let us keep in step with the Spirit. —Galatians 5:22-25 (NIV)*

EMBRACE GOD'S WORD

The Holy Spirit is God's presence with us, but how do we respond to that presence in our daily lives? We begin by embracing the Word of God. This is another way we can cultivate a life of presence.

The Spirit and the Word have a special relationship together and in relationship to believers. When Jesus spoke about the pure act of worship to God, He said that the Lord is looking for those who would worship in Spirit and in truth (see John 4:24). In John 17, Jesus prays to God for the disciples, saying, "Sanctify them in the truth; your word is truth" (John 17:17). That is a powerful picture of the unity of Word and Spirit. In John 17, the writer shows us Jesus, the Word of God, full of the Spirit of God, praying that His followers would be sanctified in the truth of the Word. Take your time with this thought. The living Word of God is praying that believers would be made holy by the Word of God Himself. The two are wed together in the life, ministry, and teaching of Jesus.

> WHEN YOU READ THE WORD AND THE SPIRIT IS WORKING THROUGH IT, YOUR HEART BECOMES FERTILE GROUND FOR THE PRESENCE OF GOD TO RESIDE.

To cultivate a life of presence, we must embrace God's Word. This means immersing ourselves in the Bible and allowing it to transform our lives. When we allow the Word to lead our path, as the psalmist says in 119:105, the presence of God is revealed in and through our lives. How is that possible? Well, if God is truth, and the Spirit reveals the truth of the Word, then when we read the Word, the truth of God is revealed to us. It is hard to cultivate something you are not aware of, especially the presence of God. When you read the Word and the Spirit is working through it, your heart becomes fertile ground for the presence of God to reside. What was once hard soil becomes a soft place for the truth of God to rest, take root, and bring forth life.

Embracing the Word of God is more than casually reading the Bible. It requires us to invite the Holy Spirit to saturate our lives with the truth of God. Every time we open the Word of God, we engage with the Spirit, soften the soil of our hearts a little bit more, and create a more viable place for the truth of God to dwell. Cultivating presence is less about the quantity of verses but rather the quality of your heart. Every believer should ask, "Is the truth of the Word of God taking root in my life, and is there evidence of that revealed through the fruit of the Spirit?" If you have not recently spent time in the Word of God, set aside a few moments this week to be still and read slowly. Don't rush. Allow each word of Scripture to breathe. If you struggle to slow down, stick with a small portion of Scripture and read slowly. You may have a personal practice of reading Scripture but have yet to learn how to respond. Before you begin reading, invite the Holy Spirit to reveal the truth of the Word and submit to His leadership as you read the text. You will start to experience God's presence in His Word and be led by the Spirit at work.

PURSUE HOLINESS

God desires for His children to be holy as He is holy. That is why He redeems creation, returning it to holiness with Him. Pursuing holiness is essential for those who long to cultivate a life of presence because it joins us with God's restorative work. If you have a new life in Christ, then that new life is already sewn into God's restorative act. Pursuing holiness is a response to the vine you are grafted into.

"But as he who called you is holy, you also be holy in all your conduct, since it is written, 'You shall be holy, for I am holy.'"—1 Peter 1:15-16

The pursuit of holiness is a willful rejection of the flesh and a pursuit of the presence of God in our lives. Holiness must be cultivated, not activated. This means it does not pop up at some point because you have become mature enough, read enough books, or pastored a large church. It must be cultivated through sanctification—the act of making something holy.

To pursue holiness, a believer must passionately long for the character of Christ to be revealed in their own life. Think of the moon's relationship to the sun. You and I can see the moon shining in the night sky because of the powerful radiance of the sun. The moon doesn't produce any light; it only reflects what it receives. In the same way, believers reflect the radiance of the Son of God. We are not holy, or even good, on our own, but we can become reflections of the glory of God. The key to pursuing holiness is to prevent anything from eclipsing the glory of God. Scripture tells us that the world does not value the holiness of God and will often criticize believers who choose to pursue Christ's values and character over the world's values. First Peter 4:4 tells us that the world considers the pursuit of holiness strange, and they will mock you as foolish. Yet, if we want a deeper life of faith, we must reject the values of the world. We must remove all sin that hinders us and pursue the pure holiness of God.

When you pray, ask the Holy Spirit to reveal any area of your life where sin has taken a foothold or become a hindrance. Be honest before the Lord with your struggles, repent of your sins, and ask Him to lead you toward holiness. If our hearts are to be good soil, we must root out the weeds of sin that would hold us back. For some, the pursuit of holiness will be crucial to whether you cultivate a life of presence. If sin is not weeded out, it will rise up and choke out the seed of the gospel in time. Pursuing holiness is a blessing because our lives become unhindered reflections of the glory of God.

PARTICIPATE IN PURE WORSHIP

Suppose it is those believers who worship in Spirit and truth who genuinely experience God's eternal presence. In that case, we must participate in worship to cultivate a life of presence. A. W. Tozer beautifully explains the historical struggle of human worship by calling it a harp that humanity had thrown into the mud. In Tozer's view, the resurrection of Christ means "That a people once made to worship Him who had lost their harp and lost their tongue and lost their desire to even worship are now caught and renewed and made alive and able to worship again."[1] A return to the presence of God is a return to the harp we have been given to worship Him. Worship and presence are intimately linked because, though the music analogy is helpful, worship is more about our life than our singing.

> **WORSHIP IS NOT ROOTED FIRST IN SINGING; IT IS FOUNDED IN THE HEART.**

Don't get me wrong—music is a powerful way to worship God, but reducing worship to one action takes away its central role in cultivating a life of presence. To worship God is to love God and bring Him something precious. Some of the earliest mentions of worship in Scripture speak directly of sacrifice. One of the most fascinating moments of Old Testament worship is in Genesis 20, when God tells Abraham to sacrifice the promised son, Isaac. There are many poignant moments in this complex passage, and there has been a great deal of discussion about what exactly God intended for this experience. What has always stood out to me is that Abraham labels this experience as worship.

---

[1] A.W. Tozer, *Whatever Happened to Worship?: A Call to True Worship* (Camp Hill, PA: WingSpread, 2012).

> *"Then Abraham said to his young men, 'Stay here with the donkey; I and the boy will go over there and worship and come again to you.'"*—Genesis 22:5

There is no mention of singing songs here, yet the reverence of worship is clearly expressed. What does this mean for those wanting to participate in worship as a way to cultivate presence? It means that worship is not rooted first in singing; it is founded in the heart. Pure worship is when we offer God what He asks for: our whole heart.

We worship God by offering every part of our lives as living sacrifices, fulfilling the greatest commandment according to Jesus: love the Lord your God with all your heart, body, and mind. Cultivating a life of presence requires you to rethink how you live. A cultivated Christian life is not a hunt for moments of presence but rather the tender care of building your life into an altar of presence. It is a response to Christ that requires our entire being.

Now, it is important to remember that worship does include singing. Worship is not reduced to singing and the making of music, but those are parts of worship that God asks for. The psalmist repeatedly commands the children of God to sing out the praises of God. Declaring the praises of the Lord is worship. There is so much that happens supernaturally when we praise: demons flee, strongholds break, hope is renewed, healing begins, and most importantly, the presence of God resides in our midst.

Worship, both song and offering, provides a residence for the presence of God, who Scripture says dwells and is enthroned upon them. So, if you are longing to cultivate a space for the presence of God, then musical praise is an incredible place to start. God is not asking you to take a lamb to a mountain for sacrifice, but He is inviting you to bring your whole heart and magnify Him in praise. This could be as simple as singing songs to Him in your prayer time, joining in corporate worship with a church congregation, or even speaking adoration to God. I encourage people to believe it is better to begin praising than wait until you have the perfect words.

Trying to figure out where to start? Open up the Psalms and simply speak them out loud. They are full of declarations of total sacrifice and are a great way to ignite worship in your life. When you cultivate that kind of soil, His presence will rest heavily, and your faith will grow.

CULTIVATE

When we spend time cultivating God's presence, something feels right. Yes, sometimes your flesh will rebel against the Spirit and say, *I don't really want to do this.* But if you submit the flesh and walk with the Spirit, you will discover the blessing of a cultivated life. You will walk this incredible journey of discovery with God Himself. If you want to begin cultivating a life of presence with God, embrace the Word of God, pursue holiness, and participate in pure worship. As you cultivate a more excellent resting place for His presence in your life, He will satisfy your soul at every level.

> *"My soul will be satisfied as with fat and rich food, and my mouth will praise you with joyful lips."*—Psalm 63:5

CULTIVATE REST

CHAPTER 4
TRUE REST

As a kid, I remember the first day off from school as the most exciting day of the year, but I am not as fired up about it as a parent. The older my kids get, the more I realize the unrealistic expectations marketed to children today. When I was a kid, the summer was a time for unregulated outdoor activity. We would wake up in the morning, go outside, and ride our bikes until the sun came down. I spent very little time expecting someone else to entertain me, especially adults. Unfortunately for my kids, their generation is under constant pressure to be entertained. There is a large cultural voice screaming, "You need this or you won't be happy." Now, this is not an attack on my kids by any means. My children are wonderful. But, overall, I have noticed a cultural pattern emerging where many kids expect a theme park experience every day. They hope to be busy, occupied, and entertained each day of summer break. The idea that any moment could be "boring" greatly offends the children. Every moment is filled with an experience, and if the experiences do not happen quickly enough, there is a screen nearby to occupy them. Now, every generation has its own issues with rest, but I am raising kids in this generation with the issues it contains. As we approached summer, I knew constant entertainment was not the right path for my kids. With that perspective in mind, my wife and I sat our oldest two kids down and told them that this summer would be about rest and balance. We would have fun, but in a way that fits into a balanced lifestyle.

It's not just children who are grappling with the concept of rest in our modern world. Our culture, too, is in a constant struggle to comprehend rest as an integral part of human life. We often reduce rest to mere napping or lounging, labeling it as lazy or unmotivated. Some even use the term to mask a selfish lack of commitment as self-care, while others view it as a repugnant symbol of a weak work ethic. These definitions, however, fail to capture the true essence of rest, and they hinder us from cultivating a healthy, restful lifestyle.

> **THE MODERN WORLD DOES NOT PRIORITIZE OR EVEN APPRECIATE HEALTHY MODES OF REST.**

The struggle of our modern culture to embrace rest is a shared experience. Almost everyone you talk to claims to be busy in some way, whether it's work, school, relationships, or life's day-to-day demands. We all know we're busy; we post about the perils of busyness and the benefits of rest, yet we rarely find the time to truly rest. A recent *Harvard Business Review* study found that now, more than ever, the business world is grappling with the concept of busyness.[2] In this article, every organization acknowledged the importance of work-life balance, yet they struggled to put that value into practice. They still sent emails at odd hours, allowed work to spill into nights, and sacrificed weekends and

---

[2] Tony Schwartz and Eric Severson, "Why We Glorify Overwork and Refuse to Rest," Harvard Business Review, 28 Aug. 2023, https://hbr.org/2023/08/why-we-glorify-overwork-and-refuse-to-rest

vacations—all things that led to burnout. Yet, despite all this, people still wear busyness like a badge of honor or token of efficiency in the marketplace. As people climbed the corporate ladder in these companies, they took more pride in wearing the "busy" badge and placed less emphasis on balance. It's no wonder that many people feel overwhelmed and frustrated. The modern world does not prioritize or even appreciate healthy modes of rest.

God did not design us to live overwhelmed and burnt out. He created us for rest. While I understand that some seasons of life are busier than others and that there are moments when a romantic sense of rest is unattainable, we must strive to cultivate a better kind of rest. This true rest is not a human invention but a divine gift rooted in God's design for us.

WHAT IS TRUE REST?

The "true rest" we speak of in this book is not the rest of the world but a rest rooted in something more significant. It is the rest of God, as revealed in the creation story in Genesis. The rest on display at creation is not a mere physical rest but a spiritual and emotional rest that comes from harmony with God's design. The rest on display at the formation of the world is this rest that we are called to cultivate in our lives:

> *Thus the heavens and the earth were finished, and all the host of them. And on the seventh day God finished his work that he had done, and he rested on the seventh day from all his work that he had done. So God blessed the seventh day and made it holy, because on it God rested from all his work that he had done in creation.* —Genesis 2:1-3

Why did God rest? Did He need a nap? Was all His power zapped, and did He need to recharge? No, of course not. God's power and might are endless. When God spoke the universe into life, He did not find it heavy work. Almighty God spoke the word, and the universe was formed. So, if He didn't need to rest, why did God take the time to rest and note it in Scripture? God rested to recognize and dwell in the glory of all He created. God's rest was not a lack of activity but a moment of reflection and appreciation.

My daughter loves to bake. Every week, she puts together a recipe for a new cookie or fancy cake I have never heard of before. One day, when I was walking through the kitchen, I watched her take a fresh batch of cookies from the oven and place them carefully on the counter. Standing on her little baking step stool, she put her hands on her hips and, with a little bounce, said, "Those are some good cookies." Creating the universe was more significant than a tray of cookies, but the response was similar. On the seventh day, God stepped back from the work of creation and partook in the glory of His creation. He looked at what He had made and called it "good." He rested like an artist who takes a moment to reflect on the beauty of what he has made. Just as the artist has his canvas, so the Master Artist, Yahweh, revels in the beauty of His creation. In that moment, as God rested to proclaim His work as good, creation declared the glory of God. From the lowest point in the ocean to the highest place in the universe, all of creation cried out to the Lord. Scripture says all creation glorifies God, and the heavens sing His praises, so at that moment, God is resting amidst the praises of all His creation and receiving the glory that comes from them.

Someone once asked me, "Who was controlling the world when God rested?" It's important to grasp that this true form of rest was not a lack of activity. God's rest was not a cessation of His authority over the universe. As Phillip Hughes aptly puts it, "Rest is not synonymous with inactivity. What God rested from was the work of creation. However, He continues to actively sustain all He has created and in the work of righteous judgment and gracious salvation."[3] God paused the work of creation to reflect on His masterpiece, and this type of rest informs our understanding of true rest for humanity. We rest not just to recharge but to reflect on and appreciate the work of our Creator, just as God did His creation. The rest of God is not just a lesson; it's a gift from God, a gift we should cherish and embrace.

REST IS A GIFT FROM GOD

God loves His creation, of which you are an essential part. In fact, He calls you beloved amongst all His creation. All His work is wonderful, but His most precious piece is you. You're a child of God. Because God loves and cares for His children, He gave them rest as a blessing. The previous chapter covered how sin destroyed the initial communion with God's presence in the garden. We were created to be in communion with God, and that included cultivating not only the garden itself but also a life at rest with the Father. Humanity lived in a perfect state of rest when they dwelled with God in the garden. That didn't mean man was without activity but rather that our souls were perfectly united with the Father. That full state of communion with God allowed

---
3 Hughes, Philip Edgcumbe. Baker Encyclopedia of the Bible. Edited by Walter E. Elwell (Grand Rapids, MI: Baker Publishing Group, 1988) 1,839. 2 vols. Baker Publishing Group, 1988.

complete rest for the souls of Adam and Eve. They could embrace the gift of rest in totality. What an incredible gift!

Rest is so important to God that He established it as an ordinance of creation. God may have cast man out of the garden, but that does not mean the need to cultivate rest disappeared. This necessary ordinance of God is established and renewed throughout the Bible, from the Old Testament to Revelation. The re-establishment of the ordinance is clearly seen when God rescues His people from Egypt and leads them toward the Promised Land. After leading them out of their slavery, He immediately renews His covenant with them and gives them the Law. God gave the Law to His people to teach them how to live in a covenant relationship with Him. Remember, God is perfect, and man is sinful. This means that there is a division in the intended communion of man and, therefore, a corruption of the rest intended for man. The Law taught how they could restore that communion through sacrifice when their sins violated the covenant. One of God's most pivotal commands was to observe the Sabbath:

> *"Remember the Sabbath day, to keep it holy. Six days you shall labor and do all your work, but the seventh day is a Sabbath to the LORD your God. On it you shall not do any work, you, or your son, or your daughter, your male servant, or your female servant, or your livestock, or the sojourner who is within your gates. For in six days the LORD made heaven and earth, the sea, and all that is in them, and rested on the seventh day. Therefore, the LORD blessed the Sabbath day and made it holy." —Exodus 20:8–11*

Sabbath is the Hebrew word for rest. God knew that because of sin, humanity would be prone to focus solely on the temporary things of the world, setting themselves up as little gods of their own lives as they worked and toiled. God is fully aware of the human condition to reject the things of eternity for the chaos and toil of the earth, so He established the Sabbath to restore the gaze of His creation toward His glory. The Sabbath day stopped the people from working, so they could give the whole focus of their hearts to God in worship. God very clearly defined this way to teach His children to cultivate rest.

The writer of Hebrews gives us an insight into the depths and richness of the Sabbath principle. When God gave Israel the Sabbath, it was a model of past, present, and future rest. The model of past rest was the foundation of rest at creation, the present being the practice and commandment of regular rest, and the future being a hope of rest finally coming through the Messiah and the coming kingdom of God.

"But as it is, they desire a better country, that is, a heavenly one. Therefore God is not ashamed to be called their God, for he has prepared for them a city."—Hebrews 11:16

The model of future rest pointed to more than a day or a promised land; it pointed to the true fulfillment of rest through the Messiah. In this way, God continually revealed His intent for rest to be restored and fulfilled. What the Jews were waiting for—what the whole earth was waiting for—was the Messiah who would establish the true rest of the kingdom.

JESUS CAME TO BE REST

The long-awaited Messiah finally came. To the surprise of the Jewish people, the Messiah did not come as they thought, and He did not do what many thought He would do. The people expected Christ would be a brave liberator when He came to be something more significant—our rest. Jesus died on the cross and defeated sin and the grave, not so that we would have access to a form of rest but that He would *be* our rest. The new life in Christ we have received is a new life in His rest. This understanding of rest changes how we read the words of Jesus in Matthew 11:

> *"Come to me, all who labor and are heavy laden, and I will give you rest. Take my yoke upon you, and learn from me, for I am gentle and lowly in heart, and you will find rest for your souls."* —Matthew 11:28-29

What kind of rest is Jesus speaking of? Is He merely offering us a good night's sleep? I remember when we adopted my son, and every night, I would sit in his room, rocking him to sleep over and over. It was a special time for us, but I prayed that God would give me some supernaturally blessed sleep. Though I appreciate that form of rest, what Jesus has to offer is far greater. The rest of Jesus is a rest in Jesus. It is a rest for our souls. When He invites the heavy laden to come to Him, the burden He speaks of is the weight of sin. Jesus invites humanity to come to Him, lay down their sins, and find true rest for their souls. But the offer is only complete with the condition of taking His yoke upon us. We have not simply come to get rest from Him but to be yoked with Him and find our rest in Him.

JESUS IS THE FULFILLMENT OF REST

We have this assurance: Jesus is the fulfillment of the human desire for rest that has been present since the fall. Jesus's work on the cross means rest and freedom from all our sins. Jesus invites us to rest right now. Our response to the glorious work of the cross is cultivating a life of rest with Jesus today.

You might think, *Wait, I know the rest of Jesus, but sometimes I don't feel at rest.* That feeling is incredibly normal for followers of Christ. When we receive new life in Christ, He invites us into His rest, but the earth will not experience complete fulfillment of rest until the second coming. What we have now is a foretaste of the immeasurably greater rest that we will all have for eternity in heaven. Jesus's works on the cross will be complete when He returns to the earth in the second coming. When His kingdom comes on earth, it will mean rest from all sorrow, pain, suffering, persecution, frustration, injustice, and death. Someday, we will experience a complete rest, but we know it in part for now. His rest is sufficient for today but will be made complete in the final days.

Praise God, who gives us rest through His Son, Jesus Christ, and invites us into a glorious eternal rest in His kingdom.

CHAPTER 5

FOLLOW THE LEADER

One year, for Mother's Day, we gave small tomato plants to all the moms in our church to bless them for all they do. It was part of a campaign to encourage mothers that all their hard work is part of nurturing a unique life. Those tomato plants weren't the blessings I thought they would be. I handed each mom the plant with a smile, only to be greeted with facial expressions of pure fear. Most moms laughed and told me the plant would die within the day. I thought they were joking, but the pictures they posted to social media later confirmed it.

I have always believed everyone can cultivate and see a plant grow. Many people claim they can't care for plants because they don't have a green thumb. I always encourage them that learning to care for plants takes time, but they will get the hang of it eventually. Looking back on that fateful Mother's Day gift, I started questioning why I believed anyone could grow anything. Why am I confident that people can cultivate and see plants grow? The answer is that I have seen it modeled.

Since I was a young kid, my mom had a garden. We would move every two years or so, yet my mom started a garden everywhere we went. She'd have my father digging holes and building boxes from sunup to sundown. I watched my parents cultivate beautiful plants in even the most unlikely spaces. Sometimes sweet potatoes covered hundreds of square feet, bringing up the healthiest tubers you have ever seen. At the same time, there were moments when the plant didn't take, bugs got into the roots, and our family learned valuable lessons on pest management. Each season, I watched and learned from what I observed.

When someone models something for us, it becomes easier to follow. Who knows what would have happened if my family had handed me a shovel and asked me to build a garden! I would have made a huge mess. But because they demonstrated it for me, I could follow their lead. The great thing about following someone's lead is that it equips you to go beyond their experience. I wouldn't dare to call myself a better gardener than my mother, but today, I can grow various plants I never even saw as a child. We can exchange seeds and take turns growing different foods. Every joy or failure is built on following what was modeled. I often look down at my dirt-covered hands and remember the first feeling of garden soil in my fingers. That dark, pungent soil connects me to the model my family taught me.

> DISCIPLESHIP MEANS TO BE WITH JESUS AND LEARN FROM JESUS HOW TO LIVE LIKE JESUS.

Many people would be completely overwhelmed if I handed them a shovel and told them to build a garden, yet many have had that happen with their faith. It might have even happened to you. Many people in the Western church discover new life in Christ, are handed a Bible by a pastor or layperson, and are told not to sin anymore. Though I appreciate the brevity of this formula, it doesn't work. This highly reductionist view of faith makes believers more stressed out than blessed. Imagine I handed you a bag of corn seed and told you that if you didn't care for this perfectly, you would starve and die. How would you feel? You'd likely be so anxious that you'd throw away the corn seed and receive whatever offer comes along instead. Many believers are anxious, hungry, and longing to follow authentic leadership.

When Christ gave you new life through Him, He did not expect you to walk it out alone. No part of our faith is a solo expedition. Christ is the model for our new life in His resurrection. He is the master teacher we follow and model every aspect of our life after. He is our teacher who leads us in the way to be; we are His disciples. Discipleship means to be with Jesus and learn from Jesus how to live like Jesus. That is the path to true spiritual maturity. Every believer must follow the teaching of Jesus and allow it to transform the way they live. In order to cultivate a life of rest, we must first become disciples of Christ, who is our rest. He is the model of our faith, and our lives are blessed and fruitful when we understand how to follow Him.

FOLLOWING THE MODEL OF REST

Jesus Christ is the model of perfect rest. Scripture tells us that what we know and have experienced in the kingdom is only part of what we will experience for eternity. When Christ returns, we will fully see the kingdom, but today, He has given us a foretaste of that kingdom. Just because we know the kingdom in part does not mean we do not have access to rest right now. Jesus Christ reveals to us how to rest even while living in this broken world. His life perfectly models the balance of rest and purpose for His disciples.

Jesus's life on earth had an evident mission and purpose. I can't imagine carrying the weight of the immense purpose God gave Jesus. Throughout the Gospels, Jesus repeatedly tells His disciples that His purpose is to do the will of the Father, which is why He had come. In the Gospel of John, Jesus says, "For this is the will of my Father, that everyone who looks on the Son and believes in him should have eternal life, and I will raise him up on the last day" (John 6:40). That is an immense purpose. When Jesus began His ministry, every day was saturated with encounters, whether they be people needing healing, confrontation with Pharisees, or miraculous works in front of crowds and disciples. Those in desperate need surrounded most places He went (see Luke 8:45). His ministry years were full of activity.

If anyone could say they were too busy to rest, it would be Jesus, yet Scripture clearly shows us He rested. I would not have blamed Jesus if He could not rest, yet He found the time. Not only did Jesus rest, but He taught His disciples to rest as well. Remember, a disciple follows the teacher's leading and allows it to change how they live. Jesus models rest, so His disciples will live it out.

At the beginning of Mark 6, Jesus sends His disciples out to neighboring cities, and Scripture tells us that they called people to repent, heal the sick, and cast out demons. As they were returning and celebrating all that had happened, the wisdom of Christ invited them immediately to rest: "And he said to them, 'Come away by yourselves to a desolate place and rest a while.' For many were coming and going, and they had no leisure even to eat" (Mark 6:31). Jesus recognized the intensity of their mission, and when they returned, He immediately invited them to rest with Him. His invitation to "come away" implies that Jesus wants His disciples to follow Him. The Master Teacher is not telling His disciples to live a way He would not live but rather inviting them to participate in a life He is modeling.

IF JESUS FULFILLED HIS CALLING AND FOUND REST, YOU CAN TOO.

Often, we hear about Jesus retreating to desolate places to pray (see Luke 5:16). It was a somewhat familiar pattern in Jesus's life. In the previously mentioned passage of Mark 6, Jesus told His disciples to come away and rest with Him, but there was one problem: the crowd following Jesus didn't get the hint. When Jesus and His disciples got to the other side of the lake to rest, they found the crowd waiting for them, ready and hungry to be fed spiritually and physically. They intended to rest, but the needs of life caught up with them. Life can be like that sometimes. As a minister, I find this to be an incredibly relatable view of Christ. It can be hard to cultivate rest when the world's demands are intense. You can have the best intentions, but life's many facets and troubles have a way of finding you. Don't be discouraged; if Jesus fulfilled His calling and found rest, you can too. It isn't always easy, but it is an essential area of our lives to cultivate if we long for more excellent spiritual health and purpose. Since the world doesn't value rest, and life will throw many things at you when you try to rest, here are some practical ways to cultivate healthy rest in your daily life.

SET HEALTHY BOUNDARIES

The first step to cultivating rest is to set healthy boundaries. We live in a world that does not prioritize good rest. You might have seen some forms of rest in culture, but are they good versions? Usually, the rest I see is "working-for-the-weekend" rest, where men and women drive themselves into the ground all week and then hope that a two-day weekend of chaotic hedonism will somehow steady their spirit for another work week. It doesn't work for most people. The other form of rest people invoke is "flaky" rest, where people quit commitments or things of actual importance when life gets challenging or even mildly inconvenient. Often, this happens because people have not set healthy boundaries in their lives. They have said "yes" to many unimportant things and become burned out with the essential things, specifically their relationship with Christ and His church.

Did you know that Jesus had boundaries? One of Jesus's boundaries was over his accessibility. There were times when Jesus was always accessible to every person from any walk of life, but there were other times when He was with a select group of disciples to pray (see Matthew 17) or even completely alone to commune with God. Mark tells us, "And rising very early in the morning, while it was still dark, he departed and went out to a desolate place, and there he prayed" (Mark 1:35). People often surrounded Jesus, but He regularly got away by Himself to pray. This boundary wasn't solely about keeping people at a distance but about drawing nearer to God. Time alone in prayer provided Christ with the space to cultivate true rest and intimate communion in the presence of God. When was the last time you got away by yourself? Now, I am not just talking about a vacation or a hike. When was the last time you got away from the overwhelming cares of the world and spent time being renewed by the presence of God? Setting boundaries on your time will allow you to cultivate a deeper faith in Christ.

Setting healthy boundaries also cultivates rest by putting our relationships in proper order. Many people need more boundaries and an appropriate order of priority in their relationships. Correct priorities are essential boundaries that every believer must establish to cultivate rest. People often give the most time and energy to relationships with the most urgent problems and the ones that demand the most attention. They frequently have no time or energy left to give to the people they care the most about, the dreams they long to fulfill, or the community they want to build. If you have felt overwhelmed in your relationships, you may have them in the wrong priority. You may not have healthy boundaries, so the most urgent troubles have stolen your energy and rest. It would help if you got your boundaries and priorities set. God must be your first priority; second is your spouse, then your family, and down from there. You might think, "I am too busy to have boundaries." You are too busy not to have boundaries. Being busy is an excellent reason to establish healthy boundaries. Even the busiest life on earth requires boundaries to allow the proper cultivation of rest. You need rest, and to cultivate that principle, you need boundaries. The demands of your life might be great, but even Jesus had boundaries on relationships. Did you know Jesus had boundaries on his family?

> *And his mother and his brothers came, and standing outside they sent to him and called him. And a crowd was sitting around him, and they said to him, "Your mother and your brothers are outside, seeking you." And he answered them, "Who are my mother and my brothers?" And looking about at those who sat around him, he said, "Here are my mother and my brothers! For whoever does the will of God, he is my brother and sister and mother." —Mark 3:31-35*

Mark doesn't describe how Mary responds to Jesus's words, but I imagine she is probably used to these responses. Raising the Son of God must have been full of a litany of unique moments. Mark shows us that Jesus prioritized relationships and was involved in the Father's work. This meant that other relationships were affected by his primary relationship to the Father and the Father's will. Jesus is not casting aside his mother or family, but He does have a clear priority of purpose. This type of boundary might sound strange to you. Remember, cultivating a life of rest requires boundaries, just as Jesus had boundaries.

We had outgrown our first little building in our sixth year as a church and felt led to sell the building and find a larger place that could facilitate all the fantastic ministry God was doing in our city. After months of prayer and searching, we found an old supermarket that had been vacant for years. When we purchased the old grocery store to convert into a church, I had no idea of the legal battle that would follow. The constant emails and phone calls back and forth absorbed every moment of my time. There would be days I would wake up at four in the morning fighting with lawyers and still be fighting at eleven o'clock at night. I distinctly remember standing in the hospital on the phone, trying to sort out legal paperwork as my wife was about to give birth to our third child. At that moment, I was frustrated at the nature of my job because I felt like it had already taken so many precious moments from me, but when I stepped back and looked, the reality was that I had not set healthy boundaries. No one was to blame but me. I had not cultivated places of rest in my own life or set healthy boundaries. I had not followed the model of Jesus Christ in my life and ministry. I could see it reflected in my family; they were suffering because I had not set healthy boundaries. Right there, I knew I had to begin cultivating a life of rest.

Setting healthy boundaries has become an incredible blessing in my life. The people I love the most respect the idea of setting boundaries. Most people are excited when they discover someone else has set boundaries because it inspires them to do the same. My job can be very demanding, but I have started setting boundaries for times I can be reached by phone. I have seen a more significant sense of peace in my own family because they know that when I am with them in that moment, nothing will steal away my affection. Setting down your phone and not going near it might sound like a small boundary, but it has a profound effect.

Take a moment and ask yourself what kind of boundaries you have. Do you have boundaries on work? Parents, do you have boundaries on technology for your children? Married couples, do you have boundaries for your parents and in-laws? We need healthy boundaries to cultivate a life of rest. A good indicator that these boundaries are not in place is that you live in constant fight or flight. If you always need to escape, you need boundaries. If you find yourself constantly abandoning the good things of life—family, church, intimacy with God—then you need to set boundaries. Setting healthy boundaries in your life is so crucial to cultivating a life of rest.

PRIORITIZE SABBATH PRINCIPLES

One time, I was speaking about the beauty of the Sabbath, and a young man came up to me at the end of the service, wanting to talk with me. He told me that the Sabbath was no longer necessary because Jesus had died and risen, and now, He is our rest. I thanked the young man for his feedback but kindly offered that he was only partly right. Jesus has indeed come to be our rest, and it is also true that Jesus has fulfilled the Sabbath, but the principle runs deeper than most people know.

Paul confirms this in his letter to the Colossians. The Colossian church was facing judgment from the Jews for their choices of food and drink, their participation in specific festivals, and their observance of the Sabbath (see Colossians 2:16-17). The judgment came from Jewish converts to Christianity who had previously lived under the law. Paul writes in his letter that the Colossians need not worry about the absence of certain feasts or particular food and drink because all those things were shadows of the substance of Jesus Christ. Paul instructs the Jewish church not to judge Gentiles because they don't recognize the Sabbath day that was under the Law. The church had received Christ, who was the fulfillment of rest, which the Sabbath was preparing the children of God for. The work of Christ is essential to modern believers' understanding of their relationship to the Sabbath.

Because of Jesus Christ, believers are not held to the lofty standard of Sabbath observation that the Jews of the old covenant were required to uphold. Jesus became for us the substance of what the Sabbath taught: rest. But there's more!

When Jesus was on the cross, he cried out, "It is finished." The death and resurrection of Jesus was a complete work that took away the sins of the world and welcomed us into His rest. Yet, if you have lived in this broken world as a believer, you have become intimately aware that the world is not entirely at rest. This world is not our final home; that reality is evident daily. The work of Christ was indeed completed on the cross, and yet we do not experience the complete fullness of it in our daily lives. Paul's letter to Corinthians reminds us that for now, we know in part and prophesy in part, but when the perfection of Jesus Christ comes, all that is known in part will pass away for the fullness of God.

Why does this matter? Well, although Christ fulfilled the Sabbath, we still need rest. You and I still live in a world without rest and must learn to cultivate rest in Jesus Christ until we die and enter eternity, or He returns in the second coming. Just because Christ fulfilled the Sabbath does not mean that humanity no longer needs time to rest. Jesus took specific time to pause His toil to get alone with God. Taking time to recover from the hectic world is integral to cultivating rest.

I know Christians who call Sunday their Sabbath. It is their way of taking a specific time out from the chaos of the world, worshipping God, and resting. It doesn't matter what day you choose to rest or how many hours you rest. What matters is that every believer takes time to cultivate rest. We must stop toiling and remember that we are not God, and the Lord is God. It is human nature to attempt to take over the position of God in our lives. Many believers think that if they take time to cultivate rest, their lives will fall apart as if the world were spinning around the force of their effort. The truth is that when we rest, the world does not end. Resting informs us that God is Lord above all, and our responsibility is to rest in Him. It is by resting in Him that we trust in Him.

> IT DOESN'T MATTER WHAT DAY YOU CHOOSE TO REST OR HOW MANY HOURS YOU REST. WHAT MATTERS IS THAT EVERY BELIEVER TAKES TIME TO CULTIVATE REST.

Take some time to think about how you could practically rest in the Lord. I remember a time in my life when I could set aside a whole day to focus on worshipping and reveling in the beauty of Jesus Christ, but that was ten years and three kids ago. I don't get a whole day to rest, but that doesn't mean I cannot engage in the principles of the Sabbath. What would a Sabbath-type moment look like for you? If you only have an hour a week, take it. Spend time worshipping the Lord and inviting the Spirit to fill you. Lean into His Word, majesty, glory, and love. However long, spend it as the children of Israel did; cease from toil, rest in the Creator, and invite the kingdom of God to manifest in your life.

DEVELOP DAILY RHYTHMS OF RENEWAL

One of the most pivotal parts of cultivating rest is developing daily rhythms of renewal. When the people of Israel were in the desert, the Lord sent them manna from heaven. This heavenly bread was their daily nourishment in a barren land and a daily reminder of God's presence with His covenant people. There was a condition on the daily bread, though: they could only keep it for one day. It was a daily provision of bread. If the people attempted to keep the bread until the next day, it became moldy and infested (see Exodus 16:19–20). When Jesus instructed His disciples on how to pray, one of the first requests He told them to make was for daily bread: "Give us this day our daily bread, and forgive us our debts, as we also have forgiven our debtors" (Matthew 6:11–12).

This language implies that the disciples of Jesus Christ must offer this prayer daily. To receive daily bread, we must request it daily. Now, I want to be careful that you don't begin to think of Jesus as some spiritual vending machine because that is different. The request for daily bread exists to cultivate a rhythm of daily communion with Christ through prayer. That simple request is a profound recognition that prayer should be more than a once-a-week moment in church but a daily rhythm of renewal with Christ. To cultivate rest, we need to create more than weekly or bi-weekly moments of communion with God; we need Him to renew us daily.

My youngest son wakes up every few hours at night right now, which means I am also waking up every few hours. It is amazing how out of touch you can be with life when you are sleep-deprived. Every area of my life becomes unsettled when I don't sleep well. My mind becomes slow, my health declines, and I get easily frustrated. Why is that? Regardless of how much we might like to compartmentalize our lives, the truth is that every part of us works together to create the whole. What might seem like a purely physical choice can affect our spiritual lives. We must recognize that our physical, emotional, intellectual, social, and spiritual health are interconnected when we cultivate daily rhythms of renewal.

Earlier, I said that rest is more than taking a nap, and while that is true, we should not disregard the importance of sleep in cultivating daily rhythms of renewal. God created us to sleep, and there are holistic consequences if we neglect it. Setting a daily sleep rhythm can be difficult in some seasons, depending on the nature of your life, but there is an excellent benefit if you are willing to try. Spending time with a close friend is another rhythm that might seem like a purely social action, yet it can be a rhythm of renewal that increases our spiritual health. Fellow believers play an essential role in building up one another's faith and standing together in suffering (see 1 Thessalonians 5:11-18; 1 Corinthians 12:26). Don't look at these rhythms of renewal and think that all you can cultivate is time in the Word of God. Your life contains many social, emotional, physical, spiritual, and intellectual facts. Take time to look at the totality of your being and think about what rhythms you can develop to help cultivate rest.

Of course, the primary rhythm believers must cultivate is centered on Jesus Christ. I have heard many suggestions about the best time to pray and read the Word, but the best time is when you take time. Have you set aside time to pray? Some religions require that their devotees pray every day at specific times. Jesus does not require that of us. You can pray anytime, but setting aside specific prayer time is helpful. Is that time more holy? Not necessarily, but it can be less interrupted, making you more renewed. Another daily renewal is time in the Word of God. God will renew you daily if you spend time reading the Word, meditating on it, or memorizing it. It is His living Word; open it anytime, and He will bless you.

> **When you abide in Him, His rest abides in you.**

Some of you may find renewal in a relationship. I praise God for the body of Christ, which facilitates this powerful aspect of faith. We can cultivate rest by praying with others in the community. As you pray with your friend, spouse, or even your kids, you will sense the pure rest of Christ. Make this a regular part of your daily rhythms. We live in a time where you can call someone a thousand miles away and pray for an hour. What a blessing that is! Whatever the daily rhythms look like for you, try something today.

When you abide in Him, His rest abides in you. Whatever daily rhythm you cultivate, do it in a restful posture. What does this mean? Try to avoid the things that distract you from cultivating rest. I was mentoring a man who repeatedly told me how he struggled to hear the voice of God. He was serving in ministry but felt burnt out and distant from God. This man was charismatic and a great communicator, but he was not renewed daily by Jesus. My advice to him was simple:

1) Be silent for ten minutes.
2) Go to a quiet place, set a timer, and sit quietly for ten minutes.
3) Don't talk, don't think through your day, and do not look at your phone.

I encouraged him just to be silent. For some of you, the first step of cultivating rest will be pausing everything and being quiet. If you cannot remember the last time you were silent for an extended period, then it might be time to cultivate a rhythm of silence. The man's problem was not that the renewing flow of Christ had ceased but that he had so much noise damming up the river. Suddenly, he began to hear from God when he sat in silence. The Word came alive to him. His prayer life was more vibrant, and most importantly, he was renewed in the rest of God.

Times in silence might be the answer for some, while for others, it might be simply giving technology a curfew at night. It may take time to find what helps you cultivate daily rhythms of renewal, but start today and start small. It is work that is worth doing. God created you and called you to rest daily in Christ, but living that life today will require cultivation.

REST WILL RESTORE YOUR SOUL

Why is there so much emphasis placed on rest? Rest restores our soul. Jesus is all about restoration. He is the Good Shepherd who came to care for us and bring us to rest. The psalmist says, "The LORD is my shepherd; I shall not want. He makes me lie down in green pastures. He leads me beside still waters. He restores my soul. He leads me in paths of righteousness for his name's sake" (Psalm 23:1–3). When Jesus rose again, He invited us into new life through Him. This new life is eternal but provides access to daily rest in Jesus Christ. Today, wherever you are, you can cultivate true rest. Because of Jesus Christ, we can dwell in the rest that brings healing and restoration. When we prioritize rest and cultivate daily rhythms that support rest, it blesses our lives and draws us deeper into the intimacy of a relationship with God. Come to Jesus, bring your weariness, and receive the rest through Him:

> *"Come to me, all who labor and are heavy laden, and I will give you rest. Take my yoke upon you, and learn from me, for I am gentle and lowly in heart, and you will find rest for your souls. For my yoke is easy, and my burden is light."* —Matthew 11:28-30

CULTIVATE AWE

CHAPTER 6

AWESOME SPLENDOR

I had never been to the Grand Canyon before moving to Arizona. One time in my teen years, my family made a trip to Phoenix to escape the rain of Washington State, and we made plans to see the Grand Canyon. We made two fateful errors on this journey, though. First, in the era before digital maps, we highly underestimated the expected five-hour journey to get there. Secondly, we had yet to learn that the northern part of Arizona is cold. No one believes me when I tell them about the climate of Northern Arizona. Try telling someone that a city in Arizona is one of the snowiest places in America, and just watch them lose their mind. We arrived in the small college town of Flagstaff dressed in our summer shorts and flip-flops and were immediately met with an all-day snowstorm. My dad decided that we had spent enough days being cold back in Washington, and we turned around and went back to the valley where the weather was consistently seventy-five degrees.

Years later, I moved to Arizona, but after three years of living in the state, I had yet to see the tremendous hole in the ground. Almost anyone I talked to was shocked and offered the same advice: "You really have to see it." Some people joked that the Grand Canyon was just another hole in the ground. I was busy planting a church then, and driving five hours to see a canyon wasn't on my list of things to do.

One day, a leader in our denomination called me up and invited me to hike the Grand Canyon. The plan was to hike down one day, camp at the bottom, and hike out the next day. That seemed easy enough to me, and the worst-case scenario was that I could officially see the hole in the ground everyone went on and on about. I was excited to finally see the canyon when we got to the ranger station. Would it live up to all my expectations, or would it fall short and be another hole in the ground? I was hopeful.

I am rarely at a loss for words, but this was one of the few times. Stepping around the bend, I caught a full glimpse of the Grand Canyon in the early morning sunlight. It was a sight that filled me with wonder. It was like how astronauts feel standing on the moon: impressed by the universe and minute in comparison. People still ask me what my first impression of it was, and the best word I can come up with is "awesome."

We can officially say that the word "awesome" has been overused. Pizza is called awesome, a vacation is described as awesome, and the birth of a child is labeled as awesome, but those certainly are not all the same level of awe-inspiring experiences. The word awesome comes from the two roots of awe, meaning great reverence or fear, and some, meaning a considerable degree. Describing something as awesome means recognizing it deserves significant or tremendous reverence and fear. The Grand Canyon is an awe-inspiring place. It is well deserving of the title "awesome." From its sheer size to its endless colors and beauty, it gives the viewer a pure sense of awe.

Standing on the edge of the Grand Canyon, I began questioning how much of my life had been spent in awe. I am highly driven, so most of my time is spent with my head down in whatever task I do. How often do I look up and stand in awe of the world around me? How frequently do I stand in awe of God? These were all the questions in my mind. I realized that I had been missing out on the beauty and wonder of life, and I made a commitment to myself to cultivate more awe in my daily life, to pause and appreciate the small miracles and grandeur of God's creation.

When was the last time you were truly in awe of something? Take a moment to reflect on a time when you were overwhelmed by the sheer magnitude of something—when words failed to capture the depth of your experience. It could be a breathtaking sunset, a powerful piece of music, or a moment of deep connection with another person. Here's a more profound question: When was the last time you were in awe of God? To cultivate a life of awe, we must start by being in awe of God. Many people have yet to realize the profound purpose and power of their new life in Christ simply because they rarely cultivate a life of awe of God. As believers, we should yearn for such a powerful encounter with God that it leaves us saying, "That's awesome."

REVERENT RECOGNITION AND FEAR

Cultivating a life of awe begins by understanding how Scripture defines it. In the Old Testament, the term comes from the Hebrew word *yārē'*. This word, used over four hundred times, is most directly translated as fear. In the New Testament, the Greek word often used is *phobos*, which you may recognize as the root of the term phobia or fear. On the surface, it may not seem like fear is the best thing to cultivate. Aren't we supposed to live without a spirit of fear?

All throughout Scripture, there is a consistent call to "fear the Lord." God is not telling His children to live in fear of Him, as we might fear spiders or clowns. Instead, it is a call to approach God with reverence and awe. So, what does the fear of God mean? At the core, fearing the Lord means sustaining a joyful, astonished awe and wonder before Him. David the psalmist says, "Let all the earth fear the LORD; let all the inhabitants of the world stand in awe of him!" (Psalm 33:8)

Rather than the fear of the Lord being a deficit in a relationship, it is a pathway to the more profound things of God. This idea is laid out in Proverbs and Psalms with great detail and repetition. Here are a few:

- Psalm 25:14: "The friendship of the LORD is for those who fear him, and he makes known to them his covenant."
- Psalm 34:7-9: "The angel of the LORD encamps around those who fear him, and delivers them. Oh, taste and see that the LORD is good! Blessed is the man who takes refuge in him! Oh, fear the LORD, you his saints, for those who fear him have no lack!"
- Psalm 111:10: "The fear of the LORD is the beginning of wisdom; all those who practice it have a good understanding. His praise endures forever!"
- Proverbs 1:7: "The fear of the LORD is the beginning of knowledge; fools despise wisdom and instruction."
- Proverbs 8:13: "The fear of the LORD is hatred of evil. Pride and arrogance and the way of evil and perverted speech I hate."
- Proverbs 14:27: "The fear of the LORD is a fountain of life, that one may turn away from the snares of death."

If you view the fear of the Lord as being afraid of God, then these verses are absolute nonsense. On the other hand, if you view it as a reverent joy in the overwhelming glory of God, then these verses will inspire you to pursue God.

Jesus told His disciples that the Father was revealed through Him. Just as the Father is revealed through the Son, Jesus Christ, so is the awe of God. Most of the "fear" or "awe" terminology in the Gospels is used to describe the astonishing works of Jesus. When Jesus heals the paralytic man and forgives his sins, Luke tells us that the crowd is filled with awe and says, "We have seen remarkable things today" (Luke 5:26, NIV). After Jesus raised the widow's son from the dead, the gathered people were said to have been filled with awe. The people responded to that awe by praising God (see Luke 7:16). Similarly, on Pentecost, when the Holy Spirit fell in tongues of fire on those believers gathered in the upper room, they gave glory to God by testifying to the truth of the gospel. Luke tells us in the Acts of the Apostles, "Everyone was filled with awe at the many wonders and signs performed by the apostles" (Acts 2:43, NIV).

When confronted by God's awesome presence, the natural human response is awe. The Bible never records a direct personal encounter with God where the individual was not visibly shaken. Think of Moses in Exodus 3 when God appears to him as the burning bush. Did that encounter not radically change Moses? The presence of God was so powerful in that desert place that Moses had to take his sandals off to approach the bush. In fact, Scripture says that Moses hid his face so that he would not see God because he was afraid. Moses was utterly in awe of God's glory, which changed his life's entire direction. The same could be said about the prophet Isaiah, who saw a mighty vision of God and the heavenly hosts. He was shaken to the point of crying out, "Woe is me!" (Isaiah 6:5) in the presence of God.

One of the most famous New Testament examples of an awe-inspiring encounter is with Saul on the way to Damascus. The glory of God was revealed so strongly to Saul that he was thrown from his donkey and blinded. The physical effects of a supernatural encounter with Jesus were life-changing (see Acts 9). That is what an authentic experience of awe can do: it radically affects how we live and approach God. Awe is unique because, when cultivated well, it becomes a powerful way to deepen our lives in Christ.

MORE THAN A FEELING

Awe is more than a feeling in a moment; cultivating it requires more than a single encounter with God. Awe is a disposition of God's people. God commanded Israel to show regard for His power and dominion and live in awe of who He is and what He does:

"Then this city will bring me renown, joy, praise and honor before all nations on earth that hear of all the good things I do for it; and they will be in awe and will tremble at the abundant prosperity and peace I provide for it."
—*Jeremiah 33:9 (NIV)*

Awe is a disposition, not just a feeling. It is a foundational mark of how the people of God live. When we cultivate awe, it produces a life fully immersed in God's presence. We live, breathe, and operate in awe of God.

Let's be honest: living in awe and cultivating a life of awe is not a common position for most people. This might be the first time you have examined the idea of the fear of the Lord or "awe." You might wonder what a life of awe even looks like or how you can begin living in awe. Recognizing awe as a crucial, reverent part of deepening our life with Christ is one thing, but it is a whole other thing to live it out. How do we cultivate awe?

To cultivate awe, we need to learn to be in awe. This begins by opening all our senses and engaging in the physical and spiritual worlds. Here are three types of awe we can engage in to cultivate it as a part of our lives.

Awe of Creation

Creation is awe-inspiring! Since I was a kid, every aspect of creation has fascinated me. I can nerd out over all kinds of things—history, motorcycles, philosophy—but nature is always the most fascinating topic. That's because the more I learn, the more I am in awe. Let me give you an example. If you have ever seen a plant, you will likely have seen a bug. Synonymous with plant growth is the reality that bugs act as pesky critters chewing away all the hard work the plant is doing. One might assume that without chemical interference, all plant life on earth faces extinction, yet that doesn't happen. How did all food survive pests for over a millennium before chemical fertilizers? The answer: the glory of creation. When plants grow up and stretch their beautiful leaves out to receive the sunshine, bugs will inevitably find them and begin to eat them. The plant can sense a bug eating it, but that's not even the best part. If the predator is part of its natural landscape, the plant will know what type of bug is assaulting it, and it sends a chemical signal that solely attracts the predator of the pesky bug. For every native, non-invasive bug like aphids or leaf-foots, a predatory insect exists to eat the initial bug. Now, I can nerd out on this for hours, but my point is that every layer of creation, even plants and bugs, should inspire awe.

God did a great job on creation. He created it magnificently because He is excellent. Modern Christians have given away the act of being in awe of creation to the hippies and new-age folks. We have allowed those who do not know the truth of God to take charge of being in reverence and awe of His creation. Unfortunately, pagan ideology will eventually lead people to replace worship of the Creator with worship of creation. Rather than recognizing the Creator and living in awe of Him, people who follow pagan ideology will begin to worship all the creation as God. The tragedy of worshipping the universe is that that form of idolatry eventually results in the destructive nature of perversion. In Paul's letter to the Romans, he instructs believers about the very truth that has been viewed in pagan societies throughout time: worshipping creation perverts the true worship our lives were meant to offer.

God made all of creation to display His glory, which should point us to Him in awe. Cultivating an awe of creation should lead us to a deeper worship of God's glory:

The heavens declare the glory of God; the skies proclaim the work of his hands. Day after day they pour forth speech; night after night they reveal knowledge. They have no speech; they use no words; no sound is heard from them. Yet their voice goes out into all the earth, their words to the ends of the world. In the heavens, God has pitched a tent for the sun. —Psalm 19:1-4 (NIV)

A. W. Tozer said that "God dwells in His creation and is everywhere indivisibly present in all His works." This is how we can worship God and not his creation.[4] For example, pagans might

---

4 A. W. Tozer, *The Pursuit of God: The Human Thirst for the Divine* (Chicago, IL: Moody Publishers, 2015).

worship the moon, and I understand how someone could be deceived into doing so. The moon is beautiful and awe-inspiring, and its presence is a unique facet of the seasons of life. The moon's glory comes from the sun; without it, it would remain dull and lifeless.

GOD'S CREATION IS RICH WITH OPPORTUNITIES TO CULTIVATE AWE OF HIM!

In the same way, all creation receives its true purpose and splendor by reflecting the glory of the Creator, Yahweh. Romans tells us that God's invisible qualities have been revealed in His creation since the beginning of the world, and they point to the truth of who He is (see Romans 1:20). God has placed His glory in the Scriptures, but He has also inscribed it on the trees of the forests and the flowers of the fields. All creation is worshipping God, and when we stand in awe of creation, we join in that worship. Go out and look at the stars, the canyons, the oceans, and the clouds, and see the glory of God on full display. This is the beauty of cultivating awe; it can be done anytime. God's creation is rich with opportunities to cultivate awe of Him!

AWE OF SALVATION

Sometimes, the reality of salvation overwhelms me. When did you last take a moment to really stop and ponder the cross? If we were honest, most of our week is likely not spent pondering Jesus's death and resurrection, and yet it is the most incredible place to stand in awe of God. This is why communion is such an important sacrament in the body of Christ. It forces us to stand in awe of the beauty and brutality of Jesus's broken body and shed blood.

> *I have been crucified with Christ and I no longer live, but Christ lives in me. The life I now live in the body, I live by faith in the Son of God, who loved me and gave himself for me.* —Galatians 2:20 (NIV)

Take a moment and dwell on that verse. Wherever you are, stop and ponder this incredible gospel. While you were dead in sin, Christ came to earth and took upon Himself all the wrath of God that should have been our judgment to suffer. Upon that rugged cross, he died under the weight of our sin and was buried in the grave. On the third day, He rose from the grave, having defeated death, and invited you to join into new life through the resurrection. Now, you have received His life today and for eternity. This is an excellent time to use the word awesome!

Pausing and sitting in awe of this profound gospel gives our lives hope. When we cultivate awe, we begin to live in a posture that says, *Thank you, Jesus, for loving and saving a sinner like me!* What would our life look like if we sat in awe of the cross daily? Would the Holy Spirit renew an awe of salvation in the church so that our lives would deepen in intimacy with God? We could spend all our lives in awe at salvation and never run out of reasons to praise the Lord. The final verse of Frederick Lehman's hymn "The Love of God is Far Greater" says it best:

> *Could we with ink the ocean fill,*
> *and were the skies of parchment made;*
> *were ev'ry stalk on earth a quill,*
> *and ev'ryone a scribe by trade;*
> *to write the love of God above*
> *would drain the ocean dry;*
> *nor could the scroll contain the whole,*
> *though stretched from sky to sky.*

AWE OF HIS PRESENCE

In the Western church, we often approach the act of worship, whether personal or corporate, as a give-and-take. It has become entirely transactional in many ways: I will bring God this if He gives me something I want. Worship partly involves bringing something to God because all true and pure worship means presenting something precious before Him, whether our praise, character, offering, or service to others. Regardless of what we bring to God, the sole purpose isn't to explicitly receive something back. In worship, we are coming to the presence of God to engage in all that He is, and the blessing of worship is that He responds generously with more of His presence. The desire of every believer should be to bring the kind of worship that honors God and draws them deeper into His presence.

One of the best descriptive views of God's presence is the glimpses of heaven in Revelation. The text of Revelation is a mix of prophetic and apocalyptic literature layered with wild visual imagery, but the consistent picture of heaven is a place of divine awe. Every creature that surrounds the throne of God lives in a continual state of awe. The winged creatures flying around the throne endlessly sing, "Holy, holy, holy," while thousands of angels declare, "Worthy is the Lamb" (see Revelation 4-5). The great multitude joins with all of heaven, later singing, "Hallelujah!" to the Lord (Revelation 19). Everyone in the presence of God worships in complete awe of God.

> WHEREVER YOU ARE RIGHT NOW, YOU CAN EXPERIENCE THE AWE OF HIS GLORY.

People say they have a list of questions to ask God when they arrive in heaven. Let's be honest; that isn't going to happen. Everyone who enters the throne room of the true and living God will be so enveloped in awe of God that their only response will be to worship Him forever and ever. They will not be a prisoner of worship but will experience God's fullness beyond all comprehension, and everything in them will erupt with praise. That is what His presence does; it is so awe-inspiring we can't help but glorify Him.

The good news is that even though we are not in heaven right now, we can still be in awe of His presence. We are blessed to have the very presence of God dwelling within us through the Holy

Spirit. When the Holy Spirit is within us, then the presence of God is with us in every moment of life. David understood this principle generations before the day of Pentecost:

Where can I go from your Spirit?
Where can I flee from your presence?
If I go up to the heavens, you are there;
if I make my bed in the depths, you are there.
If I rise on the wings of the dawn,
if I settle on the far side of the sea,
even there your hand will guide me,
your right hand will hold me fast.
—Psalm 139:7-10 (NIV)

The same God whose presence will surround us in the eternal throne room is present with us through the Holy Spirit. You don't need to enter the temple to be in His presence. Wherever you are right now, you can experience the awe of His glory. When we cultivate awe, we deepen our relationship with His presence in our lives and experience the depths and riches of our relationship with Him that go beyond our wildest expectations.

CHAPTER 7

LIFT YOUR EYES

Someone once told me that fly fishing was the hardest way to catch fish. I can think of more challenging ways, but I understand the sentiment. To many people, flyfishing makes no sense, but I have always loved it. I grew up in Washington state, where fishing is a big part of life. Like most little kids, my first introduction to fishing was with a tiny rod fitted with a random rubber lure shaped like a combination of a frog and bait fish. You could never tell what it was, but sometimes, you might get lucky with an errant cast and could reel in a small bass.

It wasn't until a family trip to Sun Valley, Idaho, that my obsession with fly fishing began. The arid landscape of eastern Idaho, with its golden hills stretching as far as the eye could see, was a stark contrast to the lush, green rivers of Western Washington. My uncle, a seasoned angler, knew all the best fishing spots in the valley, and we eagerly followed his lead. We hopped in his trusty old truck and descended the winding path to the creek near his house. He claimed that the movie *A River Runs Through It*[5] was filmed there, but since I had never seen it, I just smiled and nodded in agreement as if I knew. Once we arrived at the stream, we searched the banks to find what bugs were hatching. With our heads down, we scanned to see what the trout might be feeding on. My anticipation was building. After matching the hatch to an expertly tied fly, our eyes locked onto the water before us, searching for signs of the trout rising to eat freshly hatched hoppers or caddis.

After watching the water for a few minutes, my uncle found a good spot for me to begin casting, and I went to work. Trying my best to mimic what I had seen my dad do repeatedly, I cast my fly

---

[5] Robert Redford, *A River Runs Through It* (September 11, 1992; Culver City, CA: Columbia Pictures).

into the trickling stream and let it drift down into a deep pool. There was a long silence as the bug look-alike gently floated on the water, and then suddenly, an explosion of water. The moment a trout hits a fly is intense, like waiting in your car on the starting line and suddenly punching the gas. Everything speeds up. What was once total silence erupts into violent splashing while the cutthroat trout jumps out of the water, revealing its bright red underbelly—such a brilliant color in the beige landscape—followed by a complete sense of serenity as I released the fish back into the cool waters.

My uncle and father had gone further upstream and left me to figure this whole thing out. After more than an hour of fishing, my dad returned down the stream in my direction to make sure I was doing okay. My eyes were so locked on the water that I never saw him coming. He slowly approached me and could tell I was intensely focused. He asked me to stop fishing for a second. In this brief pause, my father gifted me the most significant phrase of fishing advice I have ever heard. He simply said, "Look up." I paused. Had I left a piece of gear behind on the bank? Was there a fish rising upstream whose signs I had totally glossed over? That wasn't it at all. My father wanted me to lift up my gaze above the water.

The trouble with fishing is that you often spend hours and hours looking down. You get to the river and look down for fish signs, down for the hatch, down to tie your gear, and down to observe the fly's path on the water. Most of the time, you walk on slippery rocks, trying not to fall and fill your waders with ice-cold water, so naturally, your head looks straight down. Standing at the base of a gigantic mountain surrounded by the most breathtaking valleys and beautiful forests, my eyes were glued to the ground. I was missing all the beauty that surrounded me. Catching fish is fun; don't get me wrong, but it is part of a more incredible experience a fisherman engages in with nature. What makes the fishing experience so powerful is not just the task of casting and catching; it is the totality of the natural world around you. The breathtaking scenery, the sights and sounds, and the ever-changing flow of the water are all part of creation's poetry in motion. Standing in a small stream in Idaho was one of the first places I learned the importance of cultivating awe.

Now, when I take people fly fishing, one of the first things I tell them is to look up. I encourage them to stop focusing so much on the task that they miss the beauty of everything surrounding them. We must train ourselves to cultivate awe in every area of our lives. When we cultivate awe, we learn to stop and observe the awe-inspiring things in our lives. It changes how we see the world and, more importantly, how we approach God and grow in our faith. A deeper faith is grown by cultivating an awe of God.

Here are a few ways cultivating awe enriches our faith.

CULTIVATING AWE LIFTS OUR HEADS

How many of us spend so much time looking down that we forget to look up? I don't mean looking at fish; I mean staring at the tasks and duties of everyday life. It is incredibly easy to fall into the rut of being entirely absorbed by the daily requirements of life. Like the rocks in the river that require a fisherman's careful gaze to navigate, many aspects of life need our attention. Life requires us, in some ways, to look at all the tasks in our path if we hope to step across them and navigate the river of life safely. Every day, some item needs our attention—jobs, finances, relationships, kids—and there is always something to navigate. What if we have been spending all our time trying not to trip, and we have missed out on standing in awe of the beauty in the world around us and the deeper purpose of our life with Christ?

> GOD HAS NOT ASKED YOU TO BEAR THE WEIGHT OF THE WORLD. HE HAS CALLED YOU TO FIND YOUR REST AND SECURITY IN HIM.

Often, we spend so much time trying not to trip on life that we are stuck with our heads down. I think about this all the time with my children. Parents, for example, can often have their heads buried in their schedule, rushing their kids from event to event, and frequently, they end up missing the awe and wonder of their children's tiny lives. People put their heads down because they have a lot to manage, but they also need to lift their heads and see the beauty of what God has given us. So many people would cultivate a life of awe if they took a second, looked up, and stood in awe of the Lord.

> *"I lift up my eyes to the hills. From where does my help come? My help comes from the LORD, who made heaven and earth."*—Psalm 121:1-2

Cultivating awe requires us to lift our eyes above our situation and circumstances. The fantastic thing is that the more you cultivate awe, the easier it is to lift your eyes. At first, looking up from everything you are navigating can be scary. What if you slip? What if you fall? A typical human fear is that we might fail at the essential things of life. Many people lie awake with their spiritual eyes buried in their worries, asking, *What if I disappoint my family?* or *What if I don't make enough money?* Those questions, unfortunately, take the whole weight of the world and put it on our shoulders.

God has not asked you to bear the weight of the world. He has called you to find your rest and security in Him. The more you stare at the worries of the world, the larger they will seem. Looking at them with anxious eyes, your troubles can transform supernaturally from a molehill to a mountain. When you take time to stop and stand in awe of God, your perspective begins to change. Lifting your eyes toward heavenly glory reminds us of God's immense power. Staring at His creation in awe informs our hearts that God is capable of so much. God is great, and we are small. He is mighty, and we are not. Yet, He loves us and is with us always.

Lay down that tension of failure and invite the Holy Spirit to lift your head to see the goodness of God all around you. Go out and stare at a mountain, river, or the stars in the heavens. Let God shape your perspective as you lift your head above the temporal struggles of the world. Cultivating awe in your life may begin by simply taking a deep breath and looking up. The advice I was given, I give to you: Look up.

CULTIVATING AWE INFORMS OUR SPIRIT

The character and nature of God inspire hope. The book of Psalms is an incredible collection of songs that recognize the glory of God. David is considered the most proficient and credited writer of Psalms, though there are other writers. When David writes to God, He professes an extraordinary recognition of the glory of God. Some Psalms are written in pain, while others are in ecstasy, yet the psalmist returns to a posture of awe each time. Even in the most anguishing pits of human suffering, David encounters the presence of God and is overcome with awe. It is this very awe that fills his spirit with hope. In times when David should be destitute, he is abundantly satisfied in his soul due to the awe of God's glory. One of my favorite writings of David is Psalm 63. David admits to being weary in flesh and spirit, yet he experiences God's glory and is renewed.

> *O God, you are my God; earnestly I seek you;*
> *my soul thirsts for you;*
> *my flesh faints for you,*
> *as in a dry and weary land where there is no water.*
> *So I have looked upon you in the sanctuary,*
> *beholding your power and glory.*
> *Because your steadfast love is better than life,*
> *my lips will praise you.*
> *So I will bless you as long as I live;*
> *in your name I will lift up my hands.*
> *My soul will be satisfied as with fat and rich food,*
> *and my mouth will praise you with joyful*
> *lips.* —Psalm 63:1-5

David's spirit, also known as his inmost being, is renewed by standing in awe of God. The deep spiritual renewal present in the glory of God is the fat and rich food David speaks of in Psalm 63. The psalmist knew the value of being in awe of God: it renews your spirit. Nothing else can renew our spirit quite like the awe of God. This humble revelation is why David says in Psalm 89:8, "Who is like you, LORD God Almighty? You, LORD, are mighty, and your faithfulness surrounds you."

David has always been passionate about sharing the remarkable character and nature of the Father. When we actively cultivate a deep sense of awe for God, we become more attuned to recognizing His extraordinary character in action. By consistently standing in awe of God, we open ourselves up to fully appreciating all of His marvelous works. As we fix our eyes and hearts on His awesomeness, we are continuously blessed with deeper insights into His boundless goodness. Embracing awe brings about a life-changing experience: we become more aware of His character at work, both within us and in the world around us.

I love being with people who are good at recognizing what God is doing. I can sometimes be very task-driven, so to cultivate awe in my life, I have prioritized spending time with people who live in awe of God. Most experienced saints of the faith have this quality present in their lives. Spend time with someone who has followed Jesus for over fifty years, and you will see how they live in awe of God. People who spend time in awe of the glory of God have a different countenance than the average person.

One of my favorite people I have ever been blessed to pastor was a woman named Paula. She knew more about the Bible than I could ever hope to learn, but beyond that, she lived in awe of

God. Paula faced all types of difficulties in life, but she repeatedly told me how God continued to renew her. When she gets overwhelmed, she just thinks about Jesus, and the awe of God strengthens her.

Those who cultivate awe are often less hurried, bothered, angered, or overwhelmed. People who cultivate awe learn to live in peace with the Lord and all that life brings. They are not tossed by the wind and waves. When life gets too big to handle, they look up to the God who created all life. They stand in awe of Him and allow Him to renew their Spirit. Cultivating awe is more than looking at nature; it is looking directly at God's glory and allowing Him to renew our Spirit.

CULTIVATING AWE INSPIRES MINISTRY

Material things in this world are not inherently evil. Living in Arizona has some benefits, including riding a motorcycle for ten out of twelve months. I love motorcycles, but they aren't everything in my life. Life becomes much less inspiring when we set our eyes, hearts, and minds only on material things.

Did you make a New Year's resolution? How long did it last? Every year, a massive portion of the population commits to budgets, fad diets, and even deep purges of random home items, but that energy doesn't last long. Eventually, the spending and weight return, and somehow, the garages and closets are fuller than the previous year. Why does this happen? Because the addition and subtraction of material and temporal pursuits is only inspiring for a short period. The possessed item may remain, but the passion they inspired no longer satisfies. Material possessions are like milk, which, when expired, is still technically milk, but now it is sour, and consuming it will not lead to satisfaction. All possessions and the joy they give have an expiration date.

When we cultivate awe, the glory of God grips our hearts, and our focus begins to shift off purely material gain. Suddenly, we look at everything from finances to schedule as an opportunity for ministry rather than a mad dash to collect the worldliest pleasures. Ministry is the work of God's kingdom that is active in our lives. The awe of God inspires a more profound ministry in our lives than simply serving in a church or nonprofit. The ministry I am speaking of transcends one church body and goes beyond the four walls of a building. Ministry means to live as Christ in the world around you everywhere you go. When the awe of God takes residence in our hearts, it naturally overflows into every part of our lives, so ministry becomes a regular operation of our lives rather than a box to check or an event to attend.

"A good man brings good things out of the good stored up in his heart, and an evil man brings evil things out of the evil stored up in his heart. For the mouth speaks what the heart is full of." —Luke 6:45 (NIV)

A heart that cultivates and is abundant in God's awe becomes a mouthpiece for God's glory. Your life begins to speak out God's glory without you saying a word. It may surprise you that God has already placed you in abundant harvest fields of ministry. The places you deem mundane might be the most poignant opportunities for ministry in your life.

The student begrudges their daily routine until they begin to see their school as a ministry and their fellow classmates as precious children of God. The office worker who views their workplace as a ministry begins to see it as a glorious place of purpose rather than a dreary necessity. Having stood in awe of God, the stay-at-home mother considers the time with her children as a faithful service to God's kingdom, even when no one else can see her diligent care.

That change in perspective can be challenging to force upon us, but when we cultivate awe, our perspective of God changes, and with it, our perspective of His kingdom at work in our lives. Living in awe of God will radically change how you approach work, marriage, parenting, family, friends, and community. What was once a place of duty will become a place of easy ministry flowing from the greater sense of God's glory in your life. What was once a struggle may begin to look like an opportunity for God to move through, for His kingdom to come, and for His will to be done on earth as it is in heaven. Get inspired by the awe of God and see how it changes your life into profound ministry.

CULTIVATING AWE GIVES US A GLIMPSE OF HEAVEN

When I was a kid, the church talked all the time about the coming glory of God. There were many songs about angels, heaven, and our eternity with Jesus. At some point, it seems like the church has shifted its focus slightly. The new generation became more concerned about the work of Jesus right now on earth than they were about the eternal glory of God. Both are crucial to informing the way we follow Christ. We need to be the hands and feet of Jesus in our communities, and at the same time, we also need the reassuring hope of the glory we will receive in heaven. The apostle Paul told the Roman church that following Christ means sharing His sufferings and glories (see Romans 8:17-18). Believers need to keep sight of both. We must actively participate in the work of Christ on earth and passionately look forward to our eternity in heaven. Having previously discussed the role cultivating awe plays in inspiring ministry on earth, we must also look at how it can give us a crucial glimpse of heaven. Cultivating a life of awe gives us a glimpse of the eternal glory we look forward to in heaven.

And we all, who with unveiled faces contemplate the Lord's glory, are being transformed into his image with ever-increasing glory, which comes from the Lord, who is the Spirit. —2 Corinthians 3:18 (NIV)

Believers in Christ have God's promise that He will take them from glory to glory. Robert Jamieson says, "As Moses's face caught a reflection of God's glory from being in His presence, so believers are changed into His image by beholding Him."[6] On earth, we experience the transformative work of God's glory as we behold Him. When we awe at God, it changes us.

The beauty of our life with Christ is that we experience the glory of God, but the tragedy of our human existence is that we will not experience the fullness of His glory until we are standing before His heavenly throne. The good news is that every believer can celebrate that they will fully realize God's glory in heaven. For centuries, Christians have taken heart in the joyous truth that there is so much glory to look forward to! Paul says that what we know and see in part today, someday, we will experience in full while standing in the presence of God (see 1 Corinthians 13:9).

---

6 David Brown, A. R. Fausset, and Robert Jamieson, Commentary Critical and Explanatory on the Whole Bible, vol. 2 (Oak Harbor, WA: Logos Research Systems, Inc., 1997), 305.

How do we get a glimpse of this heavenly glory today? When we cultivate an awe of God, we are blessed to have a taste of the glory of God on earth.

> ## DON'T GIVE GOD A LAUNDRY LIST OF REQUESTS; JUST PRAISE HIM.

In Psalm 63, David tells us how he sought God, and when he beheld the Lord's glory, he was satisfied, like the fat and rich food (see Psalm 63). In Psalm 34, David invites the reader to "taste and see that the LORD is good" (Psalm 34: 8, NIV). How often do you taste and see that the glory of God is good and satisfying? Do you find it easy to stand in awe of Him, or is it easier to simply turn the crank on religious participation? Take a moment and think about your life if you took intentional time to be in awe of God. What if your car became a place of the awe of God? What would your home look like if it became a residence of the awe of God? It would look different than it does today. If you start cultivating awe, you will be renewed in your Spirit, ignited in ministry, and see glimpses of heaven in your everyday life.

Something special happens when people lift their heads in awe of God and begin to reflect on heaven for a moment. It is as if the glory of God rests on that place for a moment in a much more significant measure. A simple exercise to cultivate awe can be gathering a few friends and praying. Don't give God a laundry list of requests; just praise Him. Declare who He is, and invite the Holy Spirit to reveal the glory of God in a fresh way. Cultivate awe and watch it deepen your life in Christ.

CULTIVATE PRAYER

CHAPTER 8

THE RESTORATION OF PRAYER

Jesus was a master teacher. A great spiritual leader once told me that one of the significant losses in Christianity is that we have learned to present the gospel without presenting Jesus as a teacher. To be a disciple of Christ is to be a follower of Christ and a student of His teachings. To follow a teacher is to be a disciple. Many opinionated definitions of discipleship have been assigned over the past few years. Still, pure and straightforward discipleship means being with Jesus and learning from Him how to live like Him. Jesus is our Savior, model, and teacher. There is a wave of voices in this world who offer to teach us, but as followers of Christ, we must listen to Him as *the* Master Teacher.

When the disciples asked Jesus how to pray, He didn't simply tell them what to pray; He taught them how to pray. Matthew 6 is one of the most straightforward and direct recordings of Jesus's teaching on how to pray. This short passage is abundantly rich in applicable teachings and life principles. On the surface, the Lord's Prayer might look like a simple list of details to be recited, but it is a transformative model that can inspire every believer to cultivate a deeper life in Christ through prayer:

> *"This, then, is how you should pray:'Our Father in heaven, hallowed be your name, your kingdom come, your will be done, on earth as it is in heaven. Give us today our daily bread. And forgive us our debts, as we also have forgiven our debtors. And lead us not into temptation, but deliver us from the evil one.'" —Matthew 6:9-13 (NIV)*

Jesus intended for the Lord's Prayer in Matthew 6 to redirect the practice of prayer away from hollow rituals and back to a pursuit of direct communion with God. The disciples whom Jesus was speaking to understood the idea of prayer to some extent. His disciples were Jewish men who had likely learned about the Law and the Prophets at a young age, and some may have learned into adulthood.

The disciples of Christ must have had a duality of experiences living in their minds. On one side was a basis of prayer from the Law and the Prophets that described how the children of Israel could commune with God. On the other hand, they witnessed the tragic way many religious leaders of the day participated in prayer. By the time of Jesus's arrival, religious leaders in Judaea had made all types of additions and changes to the act of prayer. Jesus teaches His disciples to be careful of the example of the Pharisees, who publicly used prayer for attention and glorification. Indeed, prayer had fallen far from the way God intended it.

In the Old Testament, prayer was a full petition before God. The act of prayer was often a reverent work of priestly duty, combined with an offering or sacrifice, followed by some form of petition for rescue or provision. God communed with His people through prayer. The prayers of Israel could include intercession, confession, supplication, and even praise. Israel offered these prayers to God, wanting to be covered by His favor, near His presence, and obedient to His will. The prayer Jesus teaches His disciples in Matthew 6 is rooted in the same desire for communion with God. Still, it goes deeper than the corporate ideals of prayer they previously understood.

For centuries, the people of Israel prayed to God, but to truly experience His presence, they would need the high priest to enter the holy of holies in the temple. The high priest anointed by God had to go through extensive purity rites to enter into the holy of holies and stand before the ark of the covenant where the presence of God would reside. Standing in that place, the priest could offer up the prayers of Israel to God. The ark was the place of pure communion with God. One high priest prayed to God for all Israel.

The Lord's Prayer in Matthew 6 is a significant moment in humanity's understanding of prayer. In this moment, Jesus is shifting the act of prayer from an institution to a relationship. Prayer had a new context: Jesus. He was the very presence of God manifest among them in that moment. Jesus is the High Priest who now gives all believers access to the holy presence of God. The Son of God, present at creation, came into a relationship with these disciples and taught them how to cultivate that relationship further. What had been a formulaic and somewhat distant experience for centuries was now intimately near through Immanuel—God with us. That is why Jesus preached that the kingdom of God had come near (see Matthew 4:17). The kingdom was no longer a corporate experience; it had become deeply personal to every believer. Jesus established prayer as a deeper form of communion for His followers to cultivate even long after His death and resurrection, empowering us to approach God with confidence and encouragement.

HOW TO PRAY

Earlier, we learned that Jesus is the model for all believers to follow, and in this same way, Jesus models prayer for His disciples. The wonderful thing about Jesus's presence on earth as fully man and God is that He has modeled how to cultivate a relationship with the Father through prayer. Matthew 6 is an incredible model of that prayer life. When we teach people about prayer, often the acronym we use is ACTS, which stands for adoration, confession, thanksgiving, and supplication.

Adoration

The Lord's Prayer begins with a clear adoration of recognizing God as our Father in Heaven. Matthew 6:9 says that the name of the Lord is to be hallowed, meaning to be sanctified or made holy. Each day, believers must begin their call to God in recognition of who He truly is. He is holy, worthy, and wonderful. He is deserving of all praise and adoration. If you spent your life in adoration of the character and qualities of God, you would never run out. He is an endless well of goodness worthy to be praised.

Confession

Jesus teaches His followers to seek forgiveness for their sins and to forgive the sins of others. Matthew 6:12 recognizes that each believer has received an immeasurable pardon from their sins by the blood of Christ. It also declares that Christians must choose to give grace to those who have sinned against them, just as God has generously given grace to each of us.

Thanksgiving

I usually put this second, but ATCS isn't as flashy an acronym. Thanksgiving recognizes our desire for the reality of His kingdom to manifest in this world and for all things to fall according to His will. Jesus did not instruct the disciples to pray for God's will to be molded into their own but rather that God's will would be freely and uninhibitedly manifest in their daily lives.

Supplication

The Lord's Prayer is rooted in a daily desire for the church to be led and guided by the Lord. Matthew 6:13 is a personal and corporate invitation where each believer seeks and submits to the leadership of God. Many people seek God's answers, but many more would be blessed by simply submitting to His perfect leadership.

The ACTS acronym is not a hard rule for prayer, just as the Lord's Prayer is not a command. Both forms teach believers how to pray and inform them of the general content, or "what," to pray. There are many types of prayer in Scripture and the church's history, but just like the Lord's Prayer, their explicit purpose is to teach believers how to cultivate a prayer life. Think of prayer as a whole way of living and operating in communion with God rather than one type of written praise or petition to God.

> PRAYER IS THE PURE BELIEF THAT GOD IS WHO HE SAYS HE IS AND THAT HE LONGS TO HEAR AND RESPOND TO OUR PRAYERS.

Sometimes, prayer is a petition for the blessings of redemption, such as the forgiveness of sin, sanctification, or even strength and wisdom to fulfill our Christian duties. Other times, prayer is silence and stillness before the Lord. No matter what form prayer takes, what matters is that the person praying cultivates communion with God. There are many ways to pray, and Jesus teaches His disciples to pray because prayer is essential to our new life with Him.

Throughout Scripture, prayer is the essential mode of religious life with God. Prayer is the pure belief that God is who He says He is and that He longs to hear and respond to our prayers. Even more, prayer is an act of faith, believing that God wants to work in and through the prayers His children offer Him. Prayer is more than a passing blessing over food; it is a powerful way to cultivate a deeper life of faith in Christ.

SCRIPTURE TELLS US GOD LISTENS WHEN WE PRAY

David was blessed to be called a man after God's own heart. David didn't receive that title because His life was perfect; even a surface reading of the Old Testament will reveal that. David made mistakes and had his list of failures, so how did he claim such a particular title with the Lord? He received this title because of the nature of his relationship in communion with Father God. In glory and suffering, David spoke with God.

The Psalms testify to the constant prayer of David in every season and how God listens to the prayers of His children. In Psalm 66, David says, "But God has surely listened and has heard my prayer. Praise be to God, who has not rejected my prayer or withheld his love from me!" (Psalm 66:19-20, NIV) The listening ears of God are not only tuned to the voice of David. The New Testament writers give hope to every believer today, Jew or Gentile, that God listens when we pray.

Have you ever prayed and wondered if God was listening? You may have questioned if your prayers were going up and bouncing off the ceiling. Take heart; Scripture tells us that God listens to the prayers of His children, and every believer is a child of God because of the work of Christ on the cross. Since every believer is now a son and daughter of the Almighty God, they have access to God just as David did, regardless of nationality. The apostle John, in his first letter, tells believers that they can approach Christ confidently, knowing that He hears them if they ask anything according to God's will. Have confidence that when you pray, God listens.

SCRIPTURE TELLS US GOD ANSWERS PRAYER

God not only listens to our prayers, but He also answers them. It is profoundly significant to know that God hears our prayers, but even more so, we are blessed by the truth that God answers prayers. He doesn't just listen and move on; He answers.

My children come to me with requests all the time. Sometimes, by the end of the day, I am exhausted by the number of questions a couple of children can come up with in a twenty-four-hour period. God never gets tired of our requests. He always has answers. Sometimes, my children ask me questions I don't know the answer to, or they will request things I cannot deliver, yet God is never stumped by a question, and His heavenly storeroom never runs empty. Even with my children, I listen when they ask. How odd would it be if my child came and asked me for something, I heard them out, and then just turned away and didn't respond? You might think I had lost my mind.

In the same way, when we pray, God listens and answers. He does not turn away from us. Sometimes, we get a direct answer, while other times, we are unsure of the answer or why the Lord sometimes waits to answer. However, be assured that He recognizes our requests.

We don't always know why God answers the way He does or does not answer our prayers a certain way. As a pastor, one of the questions I often get asked is why God has responded in a particular fashion or seemed not to answer. I cannot tie this issue into a simple bow, but there is a confidence every believer can possess that God will answer. Sometimes, the answer is a resounding yes; sometimes, it is a yes, but not how we anticipate, and sometimes, the answer is no. We cannot fully know the will of God beyond what the Word and the Spirit reveal to us, but we can have confidence that we serve a good God who hears and will answer our prayers: "This is the confidence we have in approaching God: that if we ask anything according to his will, he hears us. And if we know that he hears us—whatever we ask—we know that we have what we asked of him" (1 John 5:14–15, NIV).

SCRIPTURE TELLS US TO PRAY OFTEN

Since we have a God who hears and answers us, we should pray to Him regularly. If prayer is true communion with God, it is worth cultivating consistently. If God did not hear our prayers, it would make sense that prayer would seem pointless, but since

He hears and answers, we should be inspired to cultivate a consistent prayer life.

Cultivating requires consistency, so cultivating a rich prayer life requires praying often. What does consistency look like when cultivating a life of prayer? Over the millennia, religious leaders and thinkers have expressed various ideas on the frequency of Christian prayer. Since the disciples of Christ follow His model, it would be best to pray in the way Jesus did. So, how often did Jesus pray?

Jesus prayed all the time. Jesus prayed when He was alone, walking on the road, visiting with a friend, in moments of despair, preparing for a miracle, and even when He longed for His friends, the disciples, to see the true nature of the kingdom. Jesus was always praying, so believers should always pray. Pray in your car, in your house, on the way to school, driving home from work, when your kids frustrate you, when that new promotion comes through, and even when you see something beautiful and want to thank Jesus.

Pray constantly. Paul implores the Thessalonians to rejoice and pray constantly because he knows it will cultivate a rich prayer life (see 1 Thessalonians 5:16-18). Even from prison, he encouraged the church to be constant in prayer.

> *"Rejoice in hope, be patient in tribulation, be constant in prayer."*—Romans 12:12

Scripture is full of commands for Christ's followers to pray. God knows it is good for us to pray, and He put it in the Word for a reason. There have been a lot of great spiritual fathers who have blessed the church with excellent prayer practices as well. Brother Lawrence taught integrating prayer into every part of life, while Richard Foster taught how prayer is a crucial spiritual discipline believers should celebrate.[7] No matter the method, prayer is a critical area that all believers must cultivate to deepen their faith in Christ.

MORE THAN A RITUAL

What is fascinating about life is that even with the strength of Scripture, ancient church fathers, and modern leaders, praying can still be hard. All the evidence of the Word points to the glory of a cultivated prayer life, but Christians often struggle to feel like praying.

> THERE WILL ALWAYS BE A LOSS OF INTIMACY WHEN WE SHIFT PRAYER FROM BEING ABOUT JESUS TO BEING ABOUT US.

When my wife and I left Washington to move to Arizona, profound moments of prayer marked our lives. We were planting a church in a new city with a team of people who depended on us, and every day required the manifest presence of God. So, I fell on my face before God more than I ever had before. I would call out to Him, listen to the Spirit, and even sit in His

---
[7] Brother Lawerence, *The Practice of the Presence of God* (Santa Fe, NM: Martino Fine Books, 2016).

presence and find pure rest. Those prayer times were some of the deepest and richest experiences I had ever had with God. I would come out of a prayer time feeling like He had stirred up a fire in my heart.

As time passed and life became busier, I began to feel this melancholy creep in. Nothing specific was wrong, but my prayer life had become much less vibrant. I would go into my room and read the same verses, sing the same songs, and even say some of the exact words I had said for years, but suddenly, I wasn't leaving renewed like I used to. The experience had changed. You may have experienced that kind of challenging season. I started asking questions in response to this perceived dryness in my faith. I desired to find out what was wrong, so naturally, I started with me. If there is a problem, then I must be the problem. I would sit in my little room and ask God what I was doing wrong not to get the same response and experience I had before. Suddenly, I realized the problem as if God had struck my mind with lightning: I had made my prayer time about myself and ritualistic.

Those deep prayer times had started as a place to fall on my face before God, yet over time, I had become more concerned with how those times made me feel rather than how I was approaching and communing with God. There will always be a loss of intimacy when we shift prayer from being about Jesus to being about us. Feelings and experiences are good but not the foundation of our relationship with God. Prayer is more than a ritual that supplies us with a particular spiritual feeling; it is a reverent relationship we cultivate.

Some days, when I pray, my feelings do not match what I know to be true about heaven. There are still times when I go to pray and can sense a tension in my flesh. It could be because I am tired or even distracted. There are times when prayer stirs our hearts and refreshes our spirits, and there are other times when we feel out of touch with the voice of God. In those moments, every believer must make a choice. Rather than asking God's presence to submit to our feelings, we must choose to submit our feelings to the Lord. We must bring our emotions and expectations under the banner of Jesus Christ so that we might be renewed solely by His presence and leadership.

YOU HAVE HIS ATTENTION

> *"And when you pray, do not be like the hypocrites, for they love to pray standing in the synagogues and on the street corners to be seen by others. Truly, I tell you, they have received their reward in full. But when you pray, go into your room, close the door, and pray to your Father, who is unseen. Then your Father, who sees what is done in secret, will reward you. And when you pray, do not keep on babbling like pagans, for they think they will be heard because of their many words. Do not be like them, for your Father knows what you need before you ask him."*
> —Matthew 6:5-8 (NIV)

When Jesus teaches His disciples to pray, He instructs them to give their requests directly to God. This type of direct access to a divine being through prayer differs dramatically from how the Gentiles prayed to their pagan gods. Classic pagan rituals required devotees to repeatedly pray specific chants or phrases in the hopes of reaching the ears of a pagan god. Whether a monotheistic or polytheistic faith, in most ancient pagan beliefs, worshippers had to gain their god's attention. Most of the world worshipped a variety of spiritual figures who were commonly indifferent and even hostile towards human beings. It was necessary then for devotees to appease the god with an offering, gain their attention, and then make a request.

The Bible records a few of these interactions of pagan worship, specifically regarding the practices of the priests of Molech, Asherah, and Baal. One of the most famous biblical examples is in 1 Kings when Elijah challenges the prophets of Baal and Asherah to a test. Elijah would call on Yahweh, and the prophets would call on Baal. The challenge was to arouse their god with prayer chants, and whichever god answered was the true God. The prophets of Baal began the challenge. They would recite lines repeatedly as a form of divination, hoping to stir up the false god. When the repetitive prayers didn't work, the priests of Baal began cutting themselves with swords until their blood was spilled all over the dirt. Elijah began to mock them, and specifically, he poked fun at the idea that their god might be busy.

Finally exhausted and defeated, the priests of Baal stopped their repetitive shouting prayers and allowed Elijah a turn. They assumed Elijah would have the same trouble gaining God's attention. After taking the time to prepare the altar correctly, Elijah offered his prayer to God:

> *At the time of sacrifice, the prophet Elijah stepped forward and prayed: "LORD, the God of Abraham, Isaac and Israel, let it be known today that you are God in Israel and that I am your servant and have done all these things at your command.*

> *Answer me, LORD, answer me, so these people will know that you, LORD, are God, and that you are turning their hearts back again."* —*1 Kings 18:36-37 (NIV)*

Notice that Elijah's prayer was not a demand or a repetitive ritual. He did not cut himself with swords and abuse his body to gain the attention of Yahweh. His prayer contained no gnashing of teeth and screaming of incantations. It was a request of a humble servant to a loving and powerful God. He prayed this simple prayer directly to God. The elements of this simple prayer represented the kind of relationship Elijah had with God. Elijah recognized God's authority, declared God's covenant faithfulness, submitted himself as a servant of the Lord, and humbly asked for God to reveal His glory to the people of Israel and turn their hearts back to the Lord. There was no screaming, no chanting, and no need to get God's attention; Elijah already had it.

Jesus says in Matthew 6:7 (NIV), "And when you pray, do not keep on babbling like pagans, for they think they will be heard because of their many words." In this verse, Jesus is not teaching His disciples to pray concise prayers or to chastise people for having a lot to say in prayer. His issue was not with the length or repetition of the prayer but rather with the intent of worship. True prayer is more than a ritual to gain the attention of a distant God. Jesus is teaching His disciples not to babble like the prophets of Baal, hoping to get God's attention. The Lord has already given His attention to His children. Remember, the presence of God has already come near through Jesus Christ and the sending of the Holy Spirit.

Let's be honest: how often do we pray, hoping to get God's attention? Frequently, that is how we approach the Lord in prayer. We think, *I sure hope He is listening.* There have been moments in my life where deep wrestling has led me to ask God, "Are you even up there?" I don't know if I was expecting the clouds to part and reveal some supernatural realm, but I wondered if God had turned His face away from me in that lonely struggle. Many people approach prayer the same way. You wouldn't call their actions pagan, but they have the same form of divination underlining their prayers. Rather than seeing God as intimately near, they pray like they are stirring God from His slumber in the supernatural realm as if He is Batman in a cave waiting for the late-night glow of the bat signal on a cloudy sky.

> GOD IS NOT FAR FROM US; WE NEED ONLY TO TURN TO HIM.

Disciples of Jesus Christ do not need to try and get God's attention, nor should we pray in that way. God is already near, and He hears our prayer. When we draw near to God, He is close to us. James says this:

> *Come near to God, and he will come near to you. Wash your hands, you sinners, and purify your hearts, you double-minded. Grieve, mourn and wail. Change your laughter to mourning and your joy to gloom. Humble yourselves before the Lord, and he will lift you up.*
> —*James 4:8-10 (NIV)*

James is quoting very intense portions of the book of Jeremiah here, but it is a good verse when we truly understand it. Some believers have misunderstood this verse as being about God rejecting us for being imperfect, but this is untrue.

James calls believers to a continual turning and returning to Christ, similar to the parable of the prodigal son, which Jesus teaches in Luke 15. In the parable, the Father is waiting to run and embrace the lost son when the son finally repents of his ways and returns home. James is teaching in this passage that God is not far from us; we need only to turn to Him. This theological idea is consistent with what we know about Jesus, who is Immanuel—meaning God with us. We have full access to God through prayer because of Jesus Christ. We cannot conjure it up through acts of divination. It is a gift given by the grace of God and grace alone:

> *For by grace you have been saved through faith. And this is not your own doing; it is the gift of God, not a result of works, so that no one may boast. For we are his workmanship, created in Christ Jesus for good works, which God prepared beforehand, that we should walk in them.*
> —*Ephesians 2:8-10*

Take a deep breath. God has given you access to Him by His grace. There is no bat signal to light up; God has already sent out the light. When Christ was lifted up on the cross, He was the banner for all people to come under. God sent His Son to take the suffering of the world so that we might be near to Him forever. You don't need a special prayer; you need to cultivate prayer little by little today.

CHAPTER 9

FROM OVERGROWN TO OPEN

My wife and I bought our first home in 2011. It was the tail end of the market crash, and we figured this was our only shot to buy a house in Seattle. We cobbled together all the money we could, even selling our car to cover the remainder of a downpayment. The home was built in 1926 and had been with one family since 1945. Walking into the house was like stepping into an old magazine. The carpet was green shag, the countertops were burnt orange, and the windows had so many layers of paint on them you'd have better luck breaking the glass than cracking the seal.

We loved that house and all its charm. Even all these years later, it still holds a sense of romanticism to us. The house was not in the best part of town, but it still has a special spot in my heart as the place we brought home our very first baby. It was the home where I learned to build a family and started my first garden. In the rainy spring of Everett, Washington, I discovered the blessing of cultivating not only plants but a family as well.

The home's previous owner had grown old, and many general maintenance items had fallen by the wayside. The yard had once been a beautifully landscaped paradise with gardens, flowerbeds, stately vines and trellises, and even an outdoor fireplace. Over time, the gardens went to weeds, large bushes blocked out the flowerbeds, and the vines were overgrown. Another couple of years later, you could have driven by and never known a house existed. When we first viewed the house, we noticed a problem: you could not get into the backyard from the outside of the home. A massive cluster of flowering vines was between the house and the small, detached garage. You couldn't see or get past it, but it had promise. We purchased the house and started bringing it back to life.

Once the rain died down, I made my way out to the mass of vegetation to see if there was any chance of getting to the backyard from our driveway. With pruning shears in my hand, I carefully trimmed away old vines and dead leaf clusters. Minute by minute and snip by snip, the vine started to peel away and reveal something underneath. It was a gate! To my surprise, there was a gate underneath all this vine. Access to the backyard was available, but the vine had been so poorly cultivated that it had blocked off the entrance. So, I peeled back the vine, tore out the old gate and fence, put in new materials, and carefully trained the vine onto the trellis. After a couple of seasons of careful pruning and attention, what was once an absolute blockage was a beautiful doorway into the serenity of our backyard.

You may wonder what pruning a vine has to do with prayer. The idea is simple: cultivation determines accessibility. My backyard always remained in place, but the overgrown vine blocked access due to a lack of cultivation. The vine was overgrown, which gave the impression that we could not access the backyard simply because someone had not taken the time to cultivate it. Once I began cultivating the gate, it was functional and a beautiful place to access our yard.

The same principle applies to prayer. Every believer has access to God through prayer, but many are missing out due to a lack of cultivation. God is still present, but Christians have allowed features of life to overgrow and block their vision. The transformative power of prayer can clear these obstacles and bring us closer to God.

HE HAS THE PRUNING SHEERS

Every believer in Jesus Christ has access to God's presence in prayer. Nothing blocks your prayers from reaching the Father's heart. The truth is that access to God has never gone away; He will never leave you or forsake you. Because of Jesus's work, every believer can speak to the Father, providing a constant source of reassurance in their lives.

Here is the issue: when we do not cultivate prayer, it can become overgrown by other things in the world. Where there once was beautiful access to the presence of God can begin to feel distant and unclear. God has not changed positions, but other facets of our lives have overtaken the place of access. The necessities of life are not necessarily evil. Family, business responsibilities, school, and even church are good things, but just like the vine, they can creep in and take over faster than we realize.

A vine will take over if not pruned into clearly defined boundaries. I have seen beautiful vines crush a gate, burrow into a brick wall, and tear up the siding on a house. In a short while, a once proud feature of beauty can become a massive headache if not cared for properly. The gardener must prune the vine to keep it in balance.

Pruning means cutting away what the gardener believes will not lead to the fruitful and ordered growth of the plant. Jesus says in John 15:1-2, "I am the true vine, and my Father is the vinedresser. Every branch in me that does not bear fruit he takes away, and every branch that does bear fruit he prunes, that it may bear more fruit." God prunes the ones He loves so that they will bear more fruit. The Lord has the pruning shears in His hand and carefully examines the lives of those who follow Him. Notice this scripture says the Lord prunes the ones whom He loves. Pruning is always a loving act. It may seem counter to common sense for the act of "cutting away" to be a loving act, but it is the only way the life of every believer bears fruit. If we do not invite God's pruning, we may find ourselves looking around our life saying, "I think there was a gate here at one point." Remember, God's pruning is a sign of His love and care for us.

> IT'S NOT ABOUT WHAT GOD WILL DO BUT WHAT WE ALLOW HIM TO DO IN OUR LIVES.

If we want to cultivate a prayer life, we need to take responsibility and invite God to prune away what we have allowed to overgrow. For some, this could be as simple but profound as your daily schedule. You may have failed to set boundaries, allowing your calendar to overtake your spiritual life. Various life choices could fall into this category, but what matters most is that you invite the Lord to prune them away. It's not about what God will do but what we allow Him to do in our lives. Remember, by inviting God's pruning, we take an active role in our spiritual growth and transformation.

What I learned about vines is true about faith: consistency matters. Prayer is not a facet of our faith that we bulldoze into.

Whether you feel a deep sense of access to God or none, cultivating prayer takes time. We must learn how to pray and engage in these practices consistently. When we patiently and regularly cultivate prayer, it will unlock a more vibrant aspect of our faith. You can pray in these ways to begin the pruning process.

Pray in Response to God

To cultivate a life of prayer, one must first respond to God. When we pray, we respond to our unchanging heavenly Father rather than seeking to grab His attention through word or action. Prayer is a response to a powerful and loving God who has already had the first word.

John 1:1 says, "In the beginning was the Word, and the Word was with God, and the Word was God." Jesus is God's Word to us as humanity. One of the most reassuring ideas in the prayer life of believers should be that God has already reached out to us. He has already sent His Son, Jesus, the Word, to us. That very Word has given us access to God by shedding His blood. God had already had the first word.

Eugene Peterson calls prayer the second word. He says, "Prayer is never the first word; it is always the second word. God has the first word. Prayer is answering speech; it is not primarily 'address' but 'response.' Essential to the practice of prayer is to fully realize this secondary quality"[8] We don't have the first word. Christians are not the initiators of our relationship to God. We have the second word. The idea of "second word" is crucial because it sets our relationship to God in the correct order. Prayer is speaking and listening to God. Christians can engage in this relational

---
8   Eugene Peterson, *Working the Angles: The Shape of Pastoral Integrity* (Grand Rapids, MI: Eerdmans, 1989), 45-47.

communion with God because of the foundation set by Jesus Christ. I would say that fundamental to our lives as Christians is the reality that God loved first and spoke first:

> *For while we were still weak, at the right time, Christ died for the ungodly. For one will scarcely die for a righteous person—though perhaps for a good person one would dare even to die—but God shows his love for us in that while we were still sinners, Christ died for us. —Romans 5:6-8*

The faith of every Christian is a response to who God is and His love displayed in the death and resurrection of Jesus Christ. He sent the Word, Jesus Christ, to die for our sins and invite us into the resurrection. God spoke first and brought us into a relationship where we could speak second. If it is true about our whole faith, it is true about the facet of faith called prayer. We do not enter prayer as initiators but as responders. We don't carry the weight of trying to capture divine attention; instead, we respond to the Father's love. Every believer can pray in complete confidence that the same Spirit who allows us to call God our Father will be engaged in our response to His love.

Since prayer is a response to God, it should reflect gratitude for His divine providence. Cultivating a prayer life can look as simple as praising Jesus for the salvation He has given. Prayer can be as deep and profound as hours of contemplation at the foot of the cross or just gratitude for the character of God. Imagine what your life and prayers would look like if you viewed everything you did as a response to God. How would you pray differently if you genuinely believed prayer was a response to God?

> *But when the fullness of time had come, God sent forth his Son, born of woman, born under the law, to redeem*

those who were under the law, so that we might receive adoption as sons. And because you are sons, God has sent the Spirit of his Son into our hearts, crying, "Abba! Father!"
—Galatians 4:4-6

Pray With the Spirit

Praying with the Spirit might sound like a wild thought to some, but it is vital to how believers understand and commune with the triune God: Father, Son, and Holy Spirit. Every believer has access to the Holy Spirit as our advocate and counselor. When Jesus was preparing for His impending crucifixion, He comforted His disciples. They were understandably nervous at the prospect of not being physically near the Messiah they had followed for the past three years. These men had spent every moment in the very presence of Christ and now were uneasy as their Savior told them He would be leaving them to die brutally. Jesus is a compassionate Savior, and He understood the struggles of His followers.

The comfort Jesus offered His disciples was that He would send them another advocate: "And I will ask the Father, and he will give you another advocate to help you and be with you forever" (John 14:16, NIV). Notice that Jesus does not promise to send them a lesser part of God but rather "another." The Holy Spirit is another part of the Trinity but not a lesser part. Each distinct person of the Trinity makes up the totality of God. No one part is greater or lesser than the other. The Holy Spirit is God, but He is not Jesus. The advocate Jesus promises is the real presence of God manifest through the indwelling of the Holy Spirit within every follower of Christ.

The Holy Spirit is our advocate. Some translations, like the ESV, more directly translate Jesus's words in John 14:6 as "Helper." The Holy Spirit is God with us, working in and through each believer and speaking to us. Prayer is the primary way every believer in the church participates in that presence, working and talking with God.

God is already present with every believer through the Holy Spirit, and we commune with Him through prayer. That is incredibly freeing! Cultivating a life of prayer does not hinge on having the perfect words; instead, we nurture it through being attentive to the presence of a God who is already present with us, working, speaking, and moving. Paul tells the church that the Spirit will even intercede for us when we have no words to say:

In the same way, the Spirit helps us in our weakness. We do not know what we ought to pray for, but the Spirit himself intercedes for us through wordless groans. And he who searches our hearts knows the mind of the Spirit, because the Spirit intercedes for God's people in accordance with the will of God. —Romans 8:26-27 (NIV)

Paul is teaching the church that the Holy Spirit constantly intercedes for us. Why do we need the Spirit to intercede for us? In Isaiah, the Lord says His ways and thoughts are much higher than ours (see Isaiah 55:8-9). That seems like a safe bet. As someone who has surveyed my thoughts and mind, I am thankful that Yahweh's mind is infinitely greater than mine. It would be tragic if God's thoughts were at the level of our thoughts. Imagine if God was stuck on the same problems as you and me, or if He were surprised by the same issues in life—it would be embarrassing. God's thoughts and ways are so much higher than our own.

> EVEN WHEN YOUR PRAYERS ARE GROANS, THE SPIRIT TAKES THEM AND MAKES THEM A CLEAR PETITION BEFORE THE LORD.

How could we possibly know God's thoughts and ways when they are so much loftier than we could ever possess? Good news: Scripture also says that the Holy Spirit knows God's thoughts. The same Spirit who intercedes for us in our prayers knows God's thoughts and will. Whatever and however you are praying today, the Spirit is interceding. Even when your prayers are groans, the Spirit takes them and makes them a clear petition before the Lord. That should bring you comfort. There were seasons when I was so weary that all I could cultivate was prayers of groaning, but I could have hope because those prayers still reached the Father by the Holy Spirit.

Invite the Holy Spirit to work in your prayers. He will intercede even in your weakness. He knows God's thoughts. Ask the Spirit for help in prayer and listen to His leading. Regardless of how you feel as you begin cultivating a life of prayer, the Spirit is interceding for you right now:

> *Then I saw a Lamb, looking as if it had been slain, standing at the center of the throne, encircled by the four living creatures and the elders. The Lamb had seven horns and seven*

> *eyes, which are the seven spirits of God sent out into all the earth. He went and took the scroll from the right hand of him who sat on the throne. And when he had taken it, the four living creatures and the twenty-four elders fell down before the Lamb. Each one had a harp and they were holding golden bowls full of incense, which are the prayers of God's people. —Revelation 5:6-8 (NIV)*

Pray in the Name of Jesus

As a young kid, I worked all summer to buy an electric guitar because I desperately wanted to be on the worship team. There has always been something about worshipful music that enriches my heart. Even years later, when I became burned out on the politics of ministry, worship music brought me back. Church leaders had hurt me, and I was unsure about whether I would ever want to be involved in ministry again. After a while, I started attending a small church plant and sitting in the back row. Someone told them I could play guitar, and if you are familiar with how church plants work, you know I got called to join the team immediately. I wanted to avoid engaging, but a friend encouraged me to try. The music director sent me the set list, and I began practicing. Each song was about Jesus Christ. As I practiced, I sang His name over and over. I could feel the Spirit healing my heart as each verse became a musical prayer to heaven. Singing Jesus's name is why I am still in ministry today.

There has always been something about ministering to the heart of Christ through song that has profoundly affected my life. Worshipping and praying the name of Jesus is profoundly life-changing. It can heal your heart and cultivate a deeper faith. One song that often comes to mind has a beautiful chorus that over and over sings the name of Jesus Christ. This simple and powerful chorus declares that the name of Jesus is beautiful, wonderful, and powerful. No matter how many times I sing this song, each time is a powerful reminder that nothing can stand against the name of the risen King of Kings, Jesus Christ—simple lyrics with a profound truth: the name of Jesus is beautiful, wonderful, and powerful. Praying the name of Jesus is an integral part of cultivating a prayer life because it solidifies our prayer's authority on the foundation of His holy name. Just as the Spirit intercedes for us, so does Jesus Christ, though in a different way. The Holy Spirit intercedes as we pray because He knows God's thoughts. The Son also knows the will of the Father and intercedes on our behalf, but from a different posture than the Spirit. The Son intercedes at the Father's right hand, while the Spirit intercedes indwelling within the innermost being of believers. Still trying to figure it out? Let me explain.

The book of Hebrews contains an amazingly detailed explanation of Jesus's permanent priesthood. Paul most likely wrote it, though the author is unknown. Hebrews addresses a primarily Jewish audience with a historical reverence for the Levitical priesthood. In the Old Testament, the Jewish high priests were responsible for entering the holy of holies and interceding for the people's sins. The holy of holies was the most central place in the temple, where the ark of the covenant was located. The priest would enter and sprinkle the sacrificed lamb's blood on the ark. The presence of God would rest on that place, and His glory would shine through the blood, speaking to the high priest.

No one other than the high priest could ever enter behind the curtain into the holy of holies until the death and resurrection of Jesus Christ. When Jesus died upon the cross for the sins of the world, the curtain that separated the people from the holy place of God's presence was torn, and this universally significant moment changed how the children of God access His presence (see Matthew 27:51). Jesus became the access point by which believers approached the presence and the primary intercessor on our behalf:

> *Because of this oath, Jesus has become the guarantor of a better covenant. Now there have been many of those priests, since death prevented them from continuing in office; but because Jesus lives forever, he has a permanent priesthood. Therefore, he is able to save completely those who come to God through him, because he always lives to intercede for them.* —Hebrews 7:22-25 (NIV)

Jesus offered the sacrifice for humanity once and for all. He is the High Priest who will never die. When Jesus ascended to heaven, He took His rightful place at the right hand of God, where He continues to mediate and intercede on our behalf (see Romans 8:34). Just as the priests offered prayer and intercession for the people, so now does Christ intercede on behalf of our prayers to God. Everything you pray according to the will of God is wrapped in the continual intercession of Jesus.

The Holy Spirit aligns our prayers with God's will, and Jesus intercedes on our behalf—the strength and success of our prayer rest solely in the name of Jesus. Dietrich Bonhoeffer once said this about prayer:

> *Christian prayer takes its stand on the solid ground of the revealed Word and has nothing to do with vague, self-seeking vagaries. We pray on the basis of the prayer of*

the true Man Jesus Christ. . . . We can pray right to God only in the name of Jesus Christ.[9]

When we pray "in Jesus's name," we acknowledge that our faith and prayers depend entirely on Him as our Lord and Savior. Sometimes, simply speaking or singing His name can soothe a heart. There is power in the name of Jesus, not as a chant to be rehearsed but as a name to be spoken over our whole lives. His is the name above all other names. It is the name by which all are saved. It is the name we need to call on to be rescued. Praying the name of Jesus builds our faith. We do not cultivate prayer through feelings, rituals, or experience but solely on the Savior, Christ the Lord.

Pray the Word

Have you ever felt stuck in prayer? Sometimes, people will tell me they want to pray but need help knowing where to begin. They understand the glorious reality of how the Spirit and Son intercede for their prayers, but at the end of the day, they feel tongue-tied about what to say. Often, I will encourage them to say anything at all. If the Holy Spirit gives words to our groans, and Christ will intercede at the Father's right hand, then saying anything is an excellent place to start. As simple as that answer can be, there are more profound practices that can help you cultivate a life of prayer.

One practice that I have found abundantly helpful is praying the Word of God. Praying individual scriptures can be beneficial, especially in seasons when you aren't "feeling" any specific words. Maybe you have experienced these times: you go to pray, but your

---

[9] Quoted by Dietrich Bonhoeffer in Joshua Jenkin's "Bonhoeffer on the Psalter," *Every Thought Captive*, 5 January 2019, https://themajestysmen.com/joshuajenkins/bonhoeffer-on-the-psalter/.

mind struggles to know what to say. Praying the Word can soften the ground of our hearts to the reign of the Spirit.

I recommend starting with the book of Psalms. These scriptures are already a form of poetic worship, allowing a greater ease in prayer. Praying through the Psalms is a great way to start if you want to cultivate a more confident prayer life. Praying any scripture can offer a solid foundation to build on. Scripture is the living Word of God. When you pray through God's word, it comes alive in your life.

As you pray with the Word, your prayers will become less about what you bring to the table and more about your quality time in God's presence. Prayer will become less about a list of requests or needs and more about the relationship with Jesus, less about the right words and more about intimacy, less about feeling and more about revealed truth, and finally, less about experience and more about responding to God. If you are entirely new to praying God's Word, I recommend testing this practice on Psalm 23. David wrote Psalm 23 as a prayer, and its form is easy to walk through whether you have a brief or extended time. Walk the psalm verse by verse, praying each line to God and listening to how He speaks to you.

WHAT IF I DON'T FEEL IT?

Cultivating a life of prayer is one of the most precious blessings we have as a believer, but there can be times when every believer wrestles with a hunger for God's presence. There are seasons of our faith that feel drier than others. I have experienced this in my journey of faith. I encourage you that every season is different and not to be dissuaded because one moment in the journey feels different than others.

No one blames the summer for being hot or the winter for being cool. Just as life is seasonal, so is faith. Why would we expect the same feeling in every season of our faith if we would not expect the same harvest in every earthly season? Every season is different. Even in the dry season, the Holy Spirit connects you to Jesus's ongoing ministry of prayer. When we aren't feeling it, or when prayer does not deliver an experience of intimacy like we want it to, we can take heart knowing that our union with Christ is still secure.

> REMEMBER THAT REGARDLESS OF THE SEASON, YOUR FOUNDATION IS NOT YOUR EXPERIENCE; IT'S CHRIST.

When you are new to prayer, unsure of where to begin, you can trust that the same grace that rescued you is present in your prayers, and the Holy Spirit is turning even your wordless groans into fragrant offerings to heaven. When we hurt, suffer, grieve, and find it difficult to pray, we can be at peace knowing that the Holy Spirit and Jesus Christ will intercede on our behalf. Remember that regardless of the season, your foundation is not your experience; it's Christ. The Spirit is your Helper, Christ is your Mediator, and the Lord is your loving Father. We only need to speak to Him; He will hear us and answer our prayers.

CULTIVATE COMMUNITY

CHAPTER 10

COMMUNITY INCREASES GROWTH

Grow lettuce. When people ask me where to start gardening, I tell them to grow some type of lettuce. The plant is quick to germinate and requires very little observation. People usually enjoy lettuce because they only need to wait about forty days to harvest it, and it can bring about a sizeable and valuable crop. If, for some reason, it goes to seed, then you just shake the flowering heads and let the seeds fall into the ground to grow the following season.

I boasted of my lettuce-growing ability for years until one fateful season. I am unsure whether my accident came through hubris or lack of understanding, but either way, it was one of my most spectacular garden failures. I had built up multiple garden beds full of lettuce. They were indeed a pride and joy to behold—each nicely lined up with perfectly shaped lettuce heads poking out. Harvest time grew closer, and I swelled with pride.

One day, after a few warm evenings, I went out to the garden and discovered a pest had wiped out every head of lettuce. It was a complete devastation. The whole crop was gone in one weekend—I couldn't believe it. What had gone wrong? I created a mono-crop, one type of plant that was grown over and over. The issue was that when disease and pests hit one lettuce, it carried into all of them. There was nothing to stop it from spreading. My garden did not reflect the diversity of nature, which works together to keep pests and diseases from creating devastation. I had decreased diversity for production purposes, but I should have been increasing it. The garden needed companionship to thrive. It needed to be a community of plants working together rather than one type working alone.

The principle of community is woven into the fabric of the natural world. What might seem like a chaotic swirling of different natural factors is a carefully designed cooperation system. Nowhere is this more clearly revealed than in cultivation.

The modern form of agriculture is concerned primarily with mono-cropping—the act of growing one kind of crop over thousands of acres—but that isn't the principle of nature. Nature is a masterpiece of diversity, a living testament to the interconnectedness of all life. The beauty of this diversity, the way each part plays its separate role but contributes to the success of the whole, is a source of awe and inspiration. For centuries, farmers and gardeners followed the lead of the natural world and reflected these systems of companionship.

Companion planting is planting different plants that work together for their collective benefit. One of the best examples is the Three Sisters, which consists of corn, squash, and beans. Companion planting has many variations, but this simple one is a profound teacher. The squash grows big and wide as a ground cover for the slower-growing corn, keeping weeds to a minimum and shading the soil from excessive heat. The corn grows through the squash, capturing moisture from the air and supporting the beans as a trellis. The beans grow the corn, while their roots nourish the soil by increasing nitrogen. Each of these plants is entirely different. The corn from the grass family, beans from the legume family, and even the squash from the Cucurbitaceae family are all profoundly different plants, yet they work together for their benefit. The work of the other plants benefits each plant, and the collective work of nature benefits from their companionship.

In my garden, I have found this principle abundantly true. Utilizing companionship within nature is not just vital; it's a game-changer in cultivating a thriving garden. If a garden is cultivated with just one type of plant, it is more likely to fall prey to weeds, pests, and diseases. However, gardens following the companion planting model cultivate a space for each plant to support one another, bringing about a greater harvest and standing firm against potential threats.

I have often said that the garden is a great teacher. Understanding companionship in the garden has led me to appreciate better the need for every believer to cultivate community. When plants work together in a relationship, the garden has a greater chance of being healthy. When people live in a community, their faith has a more significant opportunity to be healthy. The young corn needs the squash to shade it from the heat; a new believer needs the covering of an experienced Christian to help them flourish. Believers lift each other up in faith and build up the whole body's faith in the same way that the corn supports the beans, and the soil receives the blessing of nitrogen. When cultivating a place for true companionship, you nurture the essence of human life—a deeper life in Christ.

Community is often viewed as a separate institution in the Western world. This separation of individuals and communities could be due to rampant individualism within most Western worldviews or a byproduct of "super-seized consumerism," a term used to describe the excessive and often wasteful consumption prevalent in modern societies. Whatever the reason, many people do not realize how vital community truly is. For many people, community is entirely separate from their being, when in reality, it is intimately tied into every person's life.

THE MISSING HARVEST FIELD

Every human being lives with a deep desire for relationships with other people. Very few individuals have sworn off human contact for good. Most people recognize that something is burning within us for an authentic community. We want to be known, and we want to know others. You and I were meant to have relationships with others. The Western world is now waking up to the growing deficiency of community relationships. Personal connections and community are increasingly minimal in an age where digital content is more rampant than ever. The Western world is content-rich and relationally poor. There is something profoundly personal and spiritual that is being lost due to a lack of community cultivation. Community has become the missing harvest field of our social and spiritual lives.

Technology has promised to solve the problem, but what if it is the problem? Today, the Western world's issue is that technology is partially responsible for the ever-growing rift in the connection between communities and individuals. The advent of social media promised to increase our connections, but has it done so? Has social media increased the amount of community the average person participates in or cultivates on a deeper level? No. The average person sees many people on a screen but knows very few and is known by even fewer. They are experiencing a shadow of the community they want, and no matter how much time they feed the machine, it will not satiate this burning need in their heart for community.

An app cannot fix our inherent search for connection. There is no button we can push to create relationships. Forming relationships is complex and takes endurance. Bypassing that endurance doesn't make friendships; it makes people worse at cultivating community.

Community is a vital part of our new lives in Christ but a unique place of cultivation because it is not an individual effort. You have been invited to participate in a new life with Christ through His resurrection; to cultivate that relationship, you must participate in the lives of others. Every person has a distinctive rhythm of life, with their own tendencies, schedules, and preferences. When two or more people enter a relationship, they agree to mutually pursue syncing those separate rhythms of life. Sometimes, this is an expressed agreement, but often, it is an unspoken understanding of mutual inconvenience for greater personal growth. Though both likely have packed schedules, they agree to submit their time to one another to build relationships. By laying down their monopoly on their time, they create a space for relationships to flourish. It takes time to cultivate community.

> YOUR SEARCH FOR RELATIONSHIP AND COMMUNITY BEGINS IN GOD AND IS CULTIVATED IN THE BODY OF CHRIST.

Those who have ever cultivated community know that spending quality time with people who love you is an abundant blessing, even as tricky as submitting your schedule can be. Many facets of our individual lives contribute to cultivating community, which is why it is so complex. Relationships require submitting our desires, supporting each other during hardship, forgiving the offenses of others, taking time to celebrate special moments, and, most importantly, pointing each other to the cross to receive guidance from Christ. All of this work requires patience, diligence, and a sufficient amount of grace.

There is no bypass for this process. It takes time, but the blessings far outweigh the effort. Just as the beans need the corn to stand, you need a fellow Christian to support your faith. In the same way that companionship blesses the garden, it deepens your faith. The need for community and companionship stirs deeply in your heart because you were created for it. Your search for relationship and community begins in God and is cultivated in the body of Christ.

In the beginning, God created the heavens, the earth, and everything that dwells in and on them. Finally, God created man and placed him in the garden. We have spoken in depth about man's created intent in the garden of Eden, so remember that it was the place God intended. Think about that garden again for a moment. When God forms Adam and places him in the garden, the first thing He does is set boundaries for Adam and their relationship. God's first act with mankind was relational because humanity was created for a relationship with God. It was man's primary relationship.

You may read this book and be tempted to think that the deeper faith I am describing is entirely about you, but it isn't. Thank goodness you don't have to live out your faith alone. That journey would be incredibly lonely. Instead, God has built within your nature a need for community. Cultivating a deeper faith in Christ must involve community. Community is not just lovely; it is vital to our lives as individuals and our faith as believers. God created us for it, Christ restored us to it, and we deepen our faith through it, making each individual's role in the community significant and valued.

YOU WERE CREATED FOR RELATIONSHIP

Did you know that God is inherently relational? It is woven into His whole being as a triune God: Father, Son, and the Holy Spirit. In the very beginning, God said, "Let us make mankind in our image, in our likeness, so that they may rule over the fish in the sea and the birds in the sky, over the livestock and all the wild animals, and over all the creatures that move along the ground" (Genesis 1:26, NIV). The speaker in this verse is the triune God: Father, Son, and Holy Spirit. The triune God is not speaking of man's eye or hair color here. He is speaking of man's sense of being. God created our whole being in His image. The triune God is inherently relational within Himself. He is three distinct persons in one heavenly being, meaning He is eternally and perfectly relational. When God creates man to reflect His image, it is the image of a relational God living in community with Himself. Therefore, God created man to be inherently relational in community. It has been woven into your being because it is inherent in the nature of God, who created you.

Since God made man in the image of His relational being, He also created a relationship for Adam. In the beginning, God knew that it was not suitable for man to be alone, so He made Adam a helper fit for him (see Genesis 2:18). God didn't create Eve because He was surprised that Adam needed a helper but as a continued testimony about the relational quality of mankind. God knew man required a relationship with fellow human beings, so at the very beginning, God established a standard: He created man for relationships with Himself and others. The first human beings on earth were created to be in a relationship.

Modern society has created the myth of hyper-independence, where each person is their own island, but that is a far cry from the way God created us. He did not make us hermits living alone in the woods, just as the Father is not hiding away from the Spirit somewhere in the cosmos. The Father, Son, and Spirit are intimately together in one godhead relationship. God is always in a relationship with Himself and intends for us to be in relationships with others.

YOU WERE MEANT FOR RELATIONSHIPS IN CHRISTIAN COMMUNITY

Christ's goal on earth was always to restore His people to their intended relationship with God. He spent His ministry proclaiming that the kingdom of God had come near. When Jesus began His ministry, Matthew wrote, "From that time on Jesus began to preach, 'Repent, for the kingdom of heaven has come near'" (Matthew 4:17, NIV). What does that mean? Well, the kingdom of God had come near through the manifest presence of Jesus Christ. He was fully man and fully God, and He came to take away the sins of the world. When Jesus rose from the grave, He defeated death and invited the lost children of God to return to the relationship with God they were created for. His whole mission was the restoration of His creation. He called this restored body of believers His church and bride.

> **JESUS KNEW THAT PEOPLE WERE MESSY, YET HE CHOSE TO LIVE EVERY MOMENT WITH THEM.**

The mission of Christ on earth was no small feat. It is the most important work ever done in this universe, on par with the world's creation. Christ carried a heavy purpose, yet He lived out that purpose in community. Jesus chose to have companions. If anyone could have chosen to be an island unto himself, it could have been the Son of God, yet He decided to do life with others. Not only that, but He also chose to live life with messy people.

Jesus's disciples became the most explosive force of God's glory after His resurrection, but during His ministry, they were messy, confused, and fearful, with one even betraying Him. Was Jesus not aware that people are messy? Wouldn't it have been easier if Jesus lived His ministry all alone? Of course, Jesus knew that people were messy, yet He chose to live every moment with them. Jesus understands the importance of human relationships because He was present at creation as part of the triune Godhead. Since Jesus was both fully man and God simultaneously, He is mutually expressing the image of the relational triune God and humanity created in that very God's image. Jesus is and was entirely relational. No one forced Jesus into relationships; He chose His disciples and called them friends (see John 14:16). It was His nature.

As followers of Jesus, we are called His friends. That is the foundation of His holy church. We were created for relationships; Jesus lived on earth in a relationship to restore us to a relationship with God and others. Christ made the church as His body and bride to live in relationship with Him as fellow believers. Every follower of Christ is part of the body of Christ:

Just as a body, though one, has many parts, but all its many parts form one body, so it is with Christ. For we were all baptized by one Spirit so as to form one body—whether Jews or Gentiles, slave or free—and we were all given the one Spirit to drink. Even so, the body is not made up of one part but of many. —1 Corinthians 12:12-14 (NIV)

The language Paul uses in 1 Corinthians 12 would have been well understood in the context of the Greek world. Greek thinkers often referred to the imagery of the "body" as representing a populace or community. Greeks believed that the workers were the hands that must stay active while the ruling class was the belly that must be fed to sustain the body. This short metaphor was a classic way of enforcing hierarchy and reminding the poorer class of their prescribed lesser value in Greek culture. Interestingly, Paul uses the same terminology for the body but describes an almost entirely different function. He takes a common metaphor of the day and turns it on its head. People in Greek culture thought that the body functioned because the lower social classes worked, and the better people ran the government. Where the Greek idea was meant to demote the "lesser" parts of society, Paul says that the lesser is elevated:

The eye cannot say to the hand, "I have no need of you," nor again the head to the feet, "I have no need of you." On the contrary, the parts of the body that seem to be weaker are indispensable, and on those parts of the body that we think less honorable we bestow the greater honor, and our unpresentable parts are treated with greater modesty, which our more presentable parts do not require. But God has so composed the body, giving greater honor to the part that lacked it, that there may be no division in the body, but that the members may have the same care for one another.
—1 Corinthians 12:21-25

EVERY BELIEVER IS MEANT TO BE PART OF THE BODY

The hand neither says it doesn't belong to the body because it is not a foot nor would the declaration of its insecurity determine that it did or did not have a place in the body. I would hope someone would straighten me out quickly if I started telling people that my hand was not part of my body because it was not a foot. That idea sounds foolish when we think of the human body, but what about the body of Christ called the church?

In the same way that every appendage and organ is part of the body, every single person is part of the body of Christ. Depending on your quality of self-image, you may immediately disqualify yourself from that, but you need to know that when Scripture says everyone, it means everyone. Every single believer was redeemed by Christ and restored to the community. There does not exist an equation where someone surrenders their life fully to Jesus and is not welcomed by Him into His body, that is, the church.

Now, this is not a whitewash on your experience in church. I understand that many people have past issues with feeling welcomed into the body, and that can be complicated. Some expressions of Christ's body stray from the gospel's truth. The same struggles exist today as when Paul wrote the letter to the Corinthians centuries ago. No expression of community is perfect, but that does not change the fact that you and I were created for community.

Community nourishes a deeper faith in Christ. But if we want to cultivate a life of community, we must first realize that we are part of the body of Christ. This must be known first in our hearts before it will be revealed in our habits and lifestyles.

YOU ARE AN ESSENTIAL PART OF THE BODY

Every part is different, and every part matters. In my experience, most of the struggles people have fitting in with the "church" originate in that they have been told something extra is required to be part of the body. What often happens then is that a church becomes a gathering of all one kind of body part. All over the world, we have churches made entirely of hands or churches entirely of mouths. What happens as a result is that the body is unbalanced. The church of all mouths and no ears spends all its time talking and not listening. The church without hands might be able to talk about theology until they are blue in the face, but they have never extended the love of Christ to another person. These churches are a result of human nature and fractured ideas of community where certain parts of the body are exalted, and others are called lesser.

> YOUR VALUE IN THE KINGDOM ISN'T DETERMINED BY WORLDLY VALUE; IT'S SET IN STONE BY GOD.

Paul says, "On the contrary, the parts of the body that seem to be weaker are indispensable" (1 Corinthians 12:22). Hands are great, but so are lungs and eyes. A healthy body has every part functioning in order; the same is true for the church. Cultivating community begins by recognizing that you and every believer around you are integral to the body. You are essential to the body of Christ.

Christians must cast off any false belief that some parts have value and others do not. Your value in the kingdom isn't determined by worldly value; it's set in stone by God. The culture of the kingdom is totally opposite of the world—the least is greatest, the first is last, and the last is first (see Matthew 18:1-2; 20:16). God and God alone determines our value.

The human body and the body of Christ are very similar in that the least visible parts are often the most valuable. The hands and feet are important, but how much more essential are the stomach and liver? Can a body truly function if those organs are missing? It would be challenging. Many in the church feel that if their gifts are not displayed publicly, they must not be essential, but that is not what Paul teaches. The unseen is often the most critical. Those with gifts of service, care, and hospitality are crucial to the church body. People who are quiet and diligent servants are necessary for the church's health, just as charismatic and outgoing people are. All people are essential. The body needs you.

Since everyone is necessary to the body of Christ, cultivating community involves creating space for those essential people to engage in life together. If you want to cultivate community, be the person who finds value in others as you do in yourself. We all have different minds, talents, and strengths, and we must encourage one another to build up the collective body of Christ.

WHEN THE BODY WORKS BEST

The human body is healthy when each part does what it is meant to do. In the same way, the body of Christ is at its best when all parts support each other in relationship, each doing what they were created to do. When parts of the body are not operating in total health, it is vital to do the critical work of restoring that body to full function. Cultivating community means working together to develop our communal life in the body of Christ and see it flourish.

> *"So that there should be no division in the body, but that its parts should have equal concern for each other. If one part suffers, every part suffers with it; if one part is honored, every part rejoices with it."*—1 Corinthians 12:25-26 (NIV)

Paul's inspiring image of the body of Christ is one in which each member cares for one another. If one suffers, the body suffers. If one is exalted, the body rejoices. When we begin cultivating community, our burden becomes our brothers', and theirs becomes ours. At the same time, their victory is my victory and mine theirs. One of the simplest ways to cultivate community is to support others as they pursue spiritual health. You can begin by praying with fellow believers, reading the Word together, listening to their struggles, and even cheering on their God-given dreams.

Within the Christian community, there is a mutual exchange of support and edification. Believers lay down their egos and insecurity, which try to trick them into thinking they are in competition with those around them. In turn, they experience a depth of faith unknown to the isolated individual. The foot is not in competition with the hand; you are not in competition with your fellow brother or sister in Christ. We will see a more vibrant life in Christ when we cut out competition, invest in the health of each other, and embrace cultivation.

BUILDING THE BODY GLORIFIES GOD

You might be surprised to hear that cultivating community glorifies God. We often see community as a transactional element between people, but it is worship to God. The purpose of the body of Christ is to glorify God, and when the whole body is working together, it achieves its purpose:

> *May the God who gives endurance and encouragement give you the same attitude of mind toward each other that Christ Jesus had, so that with one mind and one voice you may glorify the God and Father of our Lord Jesus Christ.*
> —Romans 15:5-6 (NIV)

Paul's charge to the early church is as relevant today as it was back then: believers glorify God when they cultivate a healthy community. The church is a collection—a body—of believers working together in a community. It can be housed in a building, but the body is more significant than a meeting place. Suppose 90 percent of your life is spent outside of a church service. In that case, it is reasonable to assume that a good portion of your time cultivating community will also exist outside a church building. I say this to encourage you to not wait for a weekend service to develop community; in fact, I would propose the opposite. Cultivating community can be the daily worship of God. Make that phone call, send that text, invite that family to dinner; it's all the active work of nurturing your life in Christ. When you cultivate this communal body of Christ, God is magnified.

Now is an excellent time to stop and review your heart. Until now, you may have been thinking of cultivating as an individual effort, but it is far more significant than that. Cultivation extends outside of every person because each believer is a part of the body. The health of your faith contributes to the health of the whole body. In the next chapter, we will discuss practical ways to cultivate community, but right now, the critical thing to remember is that you are a vital part of the body. You were created for community. Press into your created intent and cultivate community. Create a place for companionship to grow, and God will open up incredible new levels of your faith.

CHAPTER 11

THE WONDERFUL, MESSY WORK OF PEOPLE

Cultivating a garden is messy. Every gardener I have ever met proudly wore the traditional marks of humus-rich soil stretched across their face like ancient war paint. As a gardener, I have learned firsthand that cultivation is dirty work. If you were to come to my house, you would see pairs of boots caked with multiple layers of hard red dirt. Our native soil has so much clay in it that the early Pueblo tribes would stamp it into bricks and build houses, which still stand today. When it gets on your boots, it stays forever, and heaven forbid it should rain because, by the end of your gardening duties, you'll find yourself wearing platform boots made of mud. Every part of the garden clings to our person as if dragging us back into the earth from where we were formed. Even after multiple washes, my hands often have the bitter scent of freshly pruned tomato branches clinging to them. One night, my wife and I were scheduled to go out to dinner with a family in the church, but I lost track of time in the garden. When the time came to go, I was deeply involved in staking up some amaranth and digging a trench for an irrigation line. I quickly cleaned up and ran out of the house, not noticing that although my hands were clean, my face had dirt stains all around it. I looked like I had just received a cheap spray tan. It wasn't a good look.

> WORKING HARD GROUND WILL EITHER SOFTEN YOUR SPIRIT OR HARDEN YOUR SOUL.

I am not a messy person, but I do get dirty. That is what growing a crop requires: digging in your hands and getting dirty. No matter what you try to cultivate, you will get messy, likely end up scratched and bleeding, and inevitably sweaty and tired at some point. In many ways, it is expected. Cultivation requires every person to experience a myriad of emotions between the peaks and valleys. You suffer, and you celebrate. There are high highs when you see a bumper crop of tomatoes and low lows when you watch a promising peach tree give in to root rot. There are days when you are harvesting cool, crisp lettuce while the refreshing chill of the morning breeze blows through the garden and other times when you are being torn apart by one-inch thorns on a mesquite tree while one-hundred-degree heat beats down on your back. You cannot embrace one experience and reject the other. Both are required to cultivate a piece of ground properly. Each of those widely varying experiences in cultivation will teach you how to persevere.

I've heard it said that working hard ground will either soften your spirit or harden your soul. It will teach you to be soft and patient or harden you to life. If you want the harvest, you must accept the messy work of cultivation. Cultivating relationships shares the same duality of experience. There are moments when the community will refresh your spirit like a cool breeze in the garden, and there are moments when it reminds you more of the thorns on the mesquite tree, drawing blood when you least expect it. Just as a garden is beautiful and messy, so is community. Just as the blessings of a garden outweigh the mess of cultivation, so do the blessings of community, but we must be willing to get dirty. If you want to cultivate community and see the fruit of a deeper life in Christ, you must dive in and get messy. And in that mess, you will find beauty and hope.

A week before I became a lead pastor, a man I consider to be a spiritual father sat me down to share some of the wisdom he had gathered from thirty years of ministry. I was preparing for one of my life's most significant leadership shifts as I took charge of a community we had given everything to build. We were both sitting in a Scottsdale café booth sipping black coffee from dense tan mugs. I looked up from my cup and saw that he was processing how exactly to relay what he wanted to say to me. I had seen this face before on my father while growing up. It is the face of a father who wants to warn his son of the troubles ahead but not scare him away from taking the journey. With compassion on his face, he told me, "You'll have to learn to let it go."

Let what go? What had I held on to? He was referring to what people do and say to you as a minister. He told me that after decades in ministry, he still struggled to let go of the hurts that had been done to him. "It can be hard to let people go," he said, "especially when they leave messy." I have found that to be abundantly true. People are messy, and they do dirty things. The person you spend countless hours counseling and helping to restore their family will turn into your most vile enemy the following week. It is almost difficult to comprehend how vicious people can be when they truly want to be. I have led people to the Lord and helped them get clean and sober, only to have them leave the church and slander me and my family. It is a hard thing to get over. I wish I had an easy solution to get over it, but I don't. I love people, and I am willing to be honest about how much it hurts when they are messy.

Pastors don't have the market cornered on messy people. Even as you read this book, you will probably think of someone who has hurt you. Maybe it was a word they said or an action they took against you. People are messy. In fact, pastors are often very messy people themselves. We all are. We are broken and selfish and capable of all kinds of petty evils. No one is immune from causing or receiving the mess of people. So why would we want to cultivate community if the outcome can be painful? Because profound spiritual formation is only possible in a community. This means that through the challenges and joys of community life, we have the opportunity to grow spiritually, to become more like Christ, and to experience the deep joy and fulfillment that comes from living in community with others who are also on the journey of faith.

WATERING THE FIELDS OF FAITH

At one point, Maricopa County, where Phoenix metro is located, was a massive agricultural hub. Over the years, the city has undergone a dramatic change, but relics of our agrarian past still remain in intriguing forms. If you ever drive through downtown Phoenix, you might be surprised to see front yards completely flooded by four inches of water. The original irrigation canals and roads still run throughout most of the city. These canals have been around in various shapes and forms for hundreds of years, and many have been restored and expanded in the past seventy years. Flood irrigation is how many Phoenix farms and residences received water for a hundred years, and many still do today. The process is fascinating because it requires intense levels of cooperation. The canals connect each plot of land, and every person must maintain their canal so that not only their crop receives nourishment but that everyone down the line gets what they need as well. Every landowner has valves that open to allow a certain amount of water into their land and close to allow water to flow into their neighbor's land. This process requires diligence and communication. Much of the world functions in this form of communal connection. The success of each person's harvest depends on mutual stewardship of waterways and roads and the shared diligence of water usage. No one farm can stand as an isolated system because each is connected to the source of water. You simply cannot cultivate a field of corn while also ignoring the communal portion of cultivation. Getting the best harvest requires caring for canals and roads connecting each farm.

In the same way, each of these individual spiritual cultivation areas is essential, but each is united by a system that must also be diligently nurtured. Cultivating community is vital to your personal spiritual harvest. Picture a farm with multiple fields, each representing an area of cultivation: presence, awe, rest, and prayer. Now, picture canals and roads running between each of those fields, connecting them together and allowing the work of cultivation to run smoothly. Each canal brings nourishment and life to every spiritual area you cultivate. Now, picture those canals extending from your fields to your neighbors' fields, each winding into the other, bringing the nourishment to you and sending it to others—that is community. Cultivating community is how we develop the space that links all these fields together so that they can flourish in unison. It is the vital work of spiritual formation.

It is vital because, as we have said, we were created for relationships, and it is through relationships that we best nurture a deeper faith in Christ. The spiritual nourishment God sends to His people is given to the church community, of which each individual is a part. Cultivating those spaces that link us all together creates a greater ease of connection and nourishment. Cultivating a community blesses others, but it also blesses our own lives. It is not selfish to recognize that cultivating community is inherently good for your own spiritual growth.

We must do the messy work of clearing those canals and smoothing the roads between us and others. How do we go about cultivating this communal space? Here are a few ways we can begin.

Healthy Relationships Take Commitment

Remember, God created mankind to be in a relationship with Him. Yet, almost immediately, mankind chose to rebel against God. We are not robots. Each one of us was given free will to make our own choices. Now, that means humanity can choose to love God or not. Though the blessings of a loving relationship with God are infinite, time and time again, humanity has decided to rebel against God and choose sin instead.

The Lord is deeply wounded by man's sin. It is a complete violation of our communion with Him. Because humanity has turned against God, He is fully justified in His perfect judgment against the sins of mankind. Yet, God loved us so much that He sent His only son, Jesus Christ, to restore us. On the cross, Jesus took all the sins of mankind on Himself. All the horrific messiness of humanity was placed onto Jesus Christ, and the full wrath of God came against Him. Jesus willingly suffered that wrath for us so we could have a relationship with God. We have been saved and brought into communion with the Father by grace. Jesus dealt with our mess, so we could cultivate a relationship with Him and His bride, the church.

Since relationships and the work of cultivating them can be messy, we need to consistently follow Jesus's lead. When He is the cornerstone, our relationships flourish. If your commitment to nurturing community is rooted in how people treat you, it will be a short-lived effort. Eventually, someone will do something foolish and offend you. Then, your relationship will fall apart because it was based on what you received from others rather than a communal work of grace that flows from the Father God through Jesus Christ.

The reality of life is that people will offend you, and you will offend others. It is especially true of those who are closest to you. Jesus experienced this personally. Two of His closest friends turned on Him. Jesus had twelve disciples; one of them betrayed Him, and another denied Him. Judas, greedy for money, turned Jesus in to be executed. Imagine spending three years with someone, and they turn you over to be killed. Of course, Jesus knew His death and resurrection needed to be fulfilled, but Judas's betrayal still broke Christ's heart. You cannot convince me that it did not break the heart of Christ to be treated like that by a friend.

Now, picture Peter, the disciple who professed to be the most committed of all (see Matthew 26:35), but when a young servant girl questioned him, he completely denied his Master and Lord. Peter had promised to stay with Jesus to the end, defend Him against dying, and even die himself, yet Peter folded and fled when the big moment came. He was a chicken, and a rooster called him out. That is the definition of messy people. Yet, Jesus was committed to living life with people. He was committed to giving grace and raising up disciples. He did not shy away from spending time with people. If anyone could have lived out their life and faith alone, it would have been Jesus, yet He chose to live with people. In fact, the closer Jesus got to His crucifixion, the more intentional time He spent with specific people.

It takes a Christ-like commitment to cultivate community. To truly nurture a place of community, we must be committed to the work as Jesus was. He knew that relationships are vital to spiritual formation. Jesus specifically knew the blessing of friendship, that is why He purposefully called the disciples friends. Before He died, Jesus made sure that these men He had committed so much time to knew they were His friends:

"No longer do I call you servants, for the servant does not know what his master is doing; but I have called you friends, for all that I have heard from my Father I have made known to you. You did not choose me, but I chose you and appointed you that you should go and bear fruit and that your fruit should abide, so that whatever you ask the Father in my name, he may give it to you." —John 15:15-16

That is a powerful statement from our Lord and Savior. It is not the disciples who called Jesus "friend"; He called them friends. Jesus valued friendships and the role they play in faith, so He established that these men were more than servants; they were friends. They loved Him, and He loved them.

How can we follow Jesus's example and commitment?

Be Generous With Grace

Our relationship with God is founded entirely on grace. We can cultivate this relationship with Jesus because He has given us new life by grace. Since grace is the foundation of relationship with Christ, it must also be the foundation of cultivating relationships in community with others. Paul tells the Colossian church, "Bear with each other and forgive one another if any of you has a grievance against someone. Forgive as the Lord forgave you" (Colossians 3:13, NIV). Cultivating community requires extending grace even when someone offends you. To truly be generous with grace, we must be willing to give it away in abundance. Believers must quickly forgive an offense and not hold onto it anymore.

> THE EXTENSION OF GRACE TO OTHERS MUST BE A REGULAR RHYTHM OF OUR LIVES, NOT SEVEN TIMES, BUT CONTINUOUSLY.

In Matthew 18, Peter asks Jesus how many times a person should forgive a brother who sins against him. Peter offers the number seven as a solution because it is the complete number representative of God and His work. In those days, there was a rabbinical view from the Talmud stating this: "If a man commits a transgression, the first, second and third time he is forgiven, the fourth time he is not forgiven."[10] Here, Peter is more than doubling the number of times he should forgive his brother, seemingly as a devout and righteous act of grace. Yet, Jesus's response was dramatically different. Jesus responds, "I do not say to you seven times, but seventy-seven times" (Matthew 18:22). He is not challenging Peter to calculate a bigger number; He is describing a life where forgiveness is constant. Leon Morris says:

It is a way of saying that for Jesus's followers forgiveness is to be unlimited. For them forgiveness is a way of life. Bearing in mind what they have been forgiven, they cannot withhold forgiveness from any who sin against them.[11]

To cultivate community, we must be willing to forgive often and constantly. The extension of grace to others must be a regular rhythm of our lives, not seven times, but continuously.

Sometimes, people say they have forgiven but refuse to forget. Now, I am not talking about cases of abuse where boundaries must be clearly established. There are times when you can forgive someone and still find it unsafe to cultivate a relationship with them. But in the cases where brothers and sisters in Christ are offering forgiveness, we must also be quick to forget. Look at what the Word of God says about how He gives grace when our sins offend Him.

- Isaiah 43:25: "I, I am he who blots out your transgressions for my own sake, and I will not remember your sins."

---

10 Jacob Neusner, *The Babylonian Talmud: A Translation and Commentary* (Hendrickson Publishers, 2005): b. Yoma 86B, quoted in Leon Morris, *The Gospel According to Matthew* (Grand Rapids, MI: Eerdmans, 1992).
11 Leon Morris, *The Gospel according to Matthew, The Pillar New Testament Commentary* (Grand Rapids, MI: Eerdmans, 1992), 471.

- Jeremiah 31:34b: "For I will forgive their iniquity, and I will remember their sin no more."
- Psalm 103:12: "As far as the east is from the west, so far does he remove our transgressions from us."

Imagine Jesus saying that He has forgiven your sins but refuses to forget them or doesn't want you to be around Him. Would that seem like the fullness of the grace of God? Is that the kind of relationship Christ invites us into? No, of course not. Jesus taught His disciples to forgive as He has forgiven, by giving much grace (see John 6). I'm not saying that being generous with grace is easy. Nobody can offend you like the people nearest to you, but if you are quick to forgive them and abundant with grace, you are much more likely to see a harvest of the fruit of the Spirit in your relationships. Relationships that endure will bring about a great harvest of the fruit of the Spirit. Give grace and bring people near as Jesus Christ did for you.

Love Intentionally

Cultivating healthy relationships and community does not happen accidentally; it must be intentional. A good gardener or farmer prepares to plant a field. They look ahead at the seasons and pick a time that best suits their crop's growth. They carefully evaluate the seed's quality and prepare the soil with nutrients and water according to the crop's needs and nature's availability. Every facet of cultivation is intentional. When you drive through a rural area and see rows upon rows of crops, you know someone took time and effort to intentionally make that happen. Even in nature, where the growth cycles can seem random and chaotic to the casual viewer, there is actually abundant order and intent instilled into the very core by the Creator. Growth requires intentionality. Cultivating relationships requires loving intentionally.

Sometimes, it is important to step back and ask defining questions to assess how intentional we are. Where are you putting your time and energy? Is it toward relationships with Christ and others, or is it toward yourself? Are you approaching people with the love of Christ or simply to get something from them in a transactional relationship? Loving as Christ loved is the key to loving intentionally. All the love we extend to others is modeled after the love of Christ. It comes from Him:

> *"A new commandment I give to you, that you love one another: just as I have loved you, you also are to love one another. By this all people will know that you are my disciples, if you have love for one another." —John 13:34-35*

The intentional love within the Christian community is a sign to the world that we follow Christ. Note that Jesus does not say that the world will always accept the love of Christ, nor that the world's love of the church would be the metric for success, but rather that the love expressed between fellow brothers and sisters in Christ should reveal to the world who the followers of Jesus are. How does that work? Well, take the love and grace topics we have already discussed. If the church is generous with grace and intentional with love, it will look different than most of the world that does not accept those values. In a world of selfishness, vanity, and consumerism, the intentional love of believers stands as a luminous sign of our attachment to Christ. When you forgive someone and embrace them, you are revealing the love of Christ. Take a moment and ask yourself: is the way I love my fellow believers a welcome sign or a warning sign to the world around me? To cultivate community, you must love others intentionally, as Christ loved the church.

Become Fluent in Encouragement

I love being around encouraging people. I enjoy being an encourager, but also people who encourage me bless me so much. There are certain people I can't wait to call and celebrate with when something good happens. I know they will be excited about what God is doing in my life. There are other times when life gets hard, and there are certain people I can call up to be renewed. They will remind me of God's purpose for my life and encourage me not to give up. These kinds of people inspire me to encourage others. It is a blessing to have those people in your life and to be that kind of person to others.

> PEOPLE WHO EDIFY THEMSELVES MIGHT HAVE A FOLLOWING, BUT PEOPLE WHO EDIFY OTHERS HAVE FRIENDS.

For some, the language of encouragement is natural; for others, it might feel difficult or even a little uncomfortable. Learning this language of encouragement will dramatically bless your ability to cultivate community. I have noticed that encouragers always have friends. It doesn't mean you will be the most outgoing life-of-the-party member of your community, but it will mean people want to be around you. People who edify themselves might have a following, but people who edify others have friends. Paul exhorted the Thessalonians: "Therefore encourage one another and build one another up, just as you are doing" (1 Thessalonians 5:11).

Encouraging someone is a simple way to cultivate community because it builds people up. In a world that tears people down, be the kind of person who builds someone up. If you are still trying to figure out where to start, try to listen to people and hear what is happening in their lives. Find a way to remember that information—maybe write it down—and then follow up with them. Asking if you can pray for them, or even calling or texting them during the week to pray for them, can be a simple way to encourage them that goes a long way in cultivating community. Let the fruit of your lips be praise and encouragement, and watch the relationships that grow.

Seek the Holy Spirit

Let's be honest: all this hard work should not be done in our strength. If cultivating community had been left up to me, I would have burned the whole thing down and disappeared into the woods as a hermit long ago. Community is a beautiful thing that requires the Holy Spirit's continual work. We desire the Holy Spirit to be active in every aspect of our lives, so why would a community be any different? Every believer should desire the fruit of the Spirit to be present in our relationships, whether it be spouses, kids, friendships, fellow believers, or the broader community.

> *"But the fruit of the Spirit is love, joy, peace, patience, kindness, goodness, faithfulness, gentleness, self-control; against such things there is no law."*—Galatians 5:22-23

The fruit of the Spirit is a great recipe for a good relationship. Imagine if all those elements were present in your friendships. How incredible would that be? For that to be present in our relationships, we must seek the Holy Spirit. Every moment of every day must be part of a walk with the Spirit. We must surrender our strength to His leading if we desire to see His fruit cultivated in our lives. If we genuinely want to see the depths and riches of what community looks like in this new life in Christ, we need to begin cultivating it through the Holy Spirit. So much more of this life of faith is available, but it begins and ends with the Spirit of God.

A CULTIVATED LIFE

CHAPTER 12

GET YOUR HANDS DIRTY

No one becomes an expert in one day. When I started gardening, I went in with a false assumption that all my plants would live. I spent weeks carefully planting seeds, providing perfect grow lights to help them mature, and finally placing them outside. I learned almost instantly that it is more challenging than you'd think. People will tell me they don't have a green thumb because they kill plants, but I would have a black death thumb if that were true. Many people assume that cultivating a garden is a skill you either have or don't have, and though that can be true in some respects, in most cases, it isn't about natural ability but experience. The question of cultivation is whether you will be stubborn and committed enough to navigate the ups and downs or fold when the first plant fails.

Let me break the bubble right now: a plant will die. It will happen. It always happens. No matter how experienced you are, it will hurt your pride. As adults, we hate the feeling of failure. That's why many people stay the same year after year. We might have goals and resolutions, but often, we find ourselves in the same place at the end of the year as we began the year. Kids, on the other hand, are always learning. Is that just because their brains are empty, making it easier for them to soak up new information? In some ways, yes. My kids do possess an almost superhuman ability to pick up words, even if you only say them once in rush hour traffic. A child's ability to learn something new also has to do with their posture.

Kids are willing to fail. In fact, what we call failure doesn't even register in their minds. Kids don't feel foolish about trying something and failing until someone else shames them for it. Adults don't like trying new things because they don't want to look foolish. A child will learn a language and use the wrong word for something without a care in their mind. For them, using the present rather than the past tense in a conversation is not linked to their identity. Slipping in a mud puddle they are trying to cross is simply an excuse to get even dirtier, not a commentary on their physical ability. Kids don't call themselves clumsy; adults do. But to grow, we must be willing to look foolish. We must be willing to let plants die but not allow our resolve to die with them.

GROWTH IS GRADUAL, NOT INSTANT

We began our journey together by envisioning a small rectangular garden bed, full of dirt but vacant of plant life. Now, as we bring this book to a close, let's return to that image and reflect on its deeper meaning. Remember, following Jesus and living out resurrection life is more akin to cultivation than flipping a light switch. It is not something that we activate through perfect obedience or deactivate through our sins and mistakes. If that were the case, every believer would live in constant fear of messing up, and many do. Many Christians mistakenly view spiritual maturity as a streak of preventing workplace accidents, counting how many days they can go without making a mistake, and dreading the inevitable reset to day one. But true spiritual maturity and sanctification, as revealed in the Word of God, are not like that.

Our journey of living out faith is a process of cultivation called sanctification, where God continually forms us in His image. Instead of seeing spiritual maturity as an on-off switch, we've learned to view it as a garden to be cultivated. This perspective is more holistic and natural. In cultivation, the role of a believer is to nourish the soil to provide a proper resting place for the gospel to take root. Then, each believer must follow the direction of the gardener, Jesus Christ, as He shapes the plants and pulls out the weeds. Picture kneeling before the garden with Jesus. He searches the soil for what will bring a harvest of the fruit of the Spirit and begins to pull up anything that would choke it out.

This kind of work is not pass-fail. It is relational and seasonal. A deeper faith in Christ is cultivated, not forced. We must patiently and carefully follow Christ's leadership, guided by the Holy Spirit, and learn how to best steward the new life He has given us.

Throughout this book, we have discussed multiple areas believers can cultivate to deepen their faith in Christ. But remember, this transformation won't happen in a single day. You will not become an expert in cultivating a life of presence simply because you read these pages. These areas of life need to be nurtured day by day.

Reflect on your own experiences. Have you ever started a hobby and felt like you knew so much in the first week, only to look back years later and laugh at how little you actually knew? What I knew the first week of gardening felt groundbreaking to me, and it *was* at that time, but now, looking back, it seems almost funny. I felt like the king of the garden because I could grow lettuce, but now, I don't even plant lettuce seeds; I just shake the head of a sprouting plant and let it plant itself. If you remain faithful in cultivating a life in Christ, in time, you will look back and see how far you have come. What seems overwhelming now will seem simple in the future.

Here are a few final encouragements as you begin the dirty work of cultivation in your faith today:

WATCH THE SUN

I am naturally obsessive. When an idea gets into my mind, I can't shake it until I do something. My wife will laugh at all the research I do about a topic. Some people research to ensure they know every angle before they begin; I do research while my hands are already in the mess. My whole life becomes wrapped in whatever task I face. The problem with that approach is that sometimes you leap before you look.

> THE MOST IMPORTANT PART OF CULTIVATING YOUR FAITH IS LOOKING AT JESUS, GOD'S SON.

One year, I wanted to grow some amaranth in my yard. I found a good spot in the yard with the right balance of sunlight and shade. We must pay attention to how much sunshine a plant gets in Arizona because four hours here feels like ten in Washington. Once I found the spot, I built a garden bed and started planting. Week after week went by, but instead of a harvest, I had a problem. I should have paid more attention to the changing of the sun between seasons. What had been a sunny area when I started was now entirely shaded by a roof line all day because of the different positions of the sun in the sky. If I had taken the time to watch the sun in the sky over time, I would have known that this place would not foster the best growth in this season, but I was impatient. I was so eager to build the garden that I neglected to look at the sun.

As you cultivate a deeper faith in Christ, look at the Son. The shining glory of God for our lives is more than a ball of gaseous fire millions of miles away; it is our Lord and Savior, Jesus Christ. If you are reading this book, you might feel a tension in your spirit to start putting a hand to plow in your spiritual life, but pause first. The most important part of cultivating your faith is looking at Jesus, God's Son. This whole life we have received is rooted in Him, and it is to Him that we must all look for guidance. I hope everyone who reads this book on cultivation goes into a quiet place, falls on their face before Jesus, and invites Him to lead them. The temptation is to read a book on cultivation and look inward, but I want to encourage you to look to Jesus to speak to your innermost being. Where is Jesus leading you? Where is He telling you to cultivate? Take a deep breath, slow down, seek Him in prayer, and trust He will speak to you.

START DIGGING

Prepping for planting season is always a fun process. The counter becomes littered with dozens of seed packets, each adorned with bright images of each seed's most successful possibility. The smell of rich soil permeates the kitchen as my kids fill seed trays, and I try my best to keep the dirt explosion to a minimum. All this preparation eventually leads to a logical conclusion: it is time to start digging. No matter how much theoretical work and preparation you put in, at some point, you must grab a shovel and start digging. You must get dirty.

Sometimes, it is easier for our faith to live in a theoretical space. It is safe there, isn't challenged, and can't get messy. When our faith moves from our heads to our hearts and hands, it becomes a grander experience. No matter how many books you read, how many times you read this book, and how many conferences you attend, eventually, you will need to start digging if you want your faith to grow. As someone who has spent a lot of time wrestling with cultivating his faith, let me encourage you to plan some specific time for this dirt work. It will take time and energy and will not happen accidentally. Give thought to when you will do the job of cultivating the areas Jesus directs you in. Will it be the morning before work, on the way to work, or before bed? Pick a time; if it doesn't work, just pick another time. You won't know the perfect time until you start digging. Don't let an insecurity about the right time derail your beginning; just start digging.

START SMALL

People sometimes ask me where to start gardening, and my answer is always the same: start small. Get a small planter and one tomato plant, and if you are feeling brave, get some lettuce. That will keep you occupied for a season, trust me. Yet, even with that advice, people always start big. It must be human nature that we think starting bigger will make us an expert sooner— some kind of fake-it-until-you-make-it ideology, I guess—but it isn't true. People will build massive garden beds with twelve different varieties of carrots and then call me asking why they aren't growing. I usually tell them I have no idea; I am not an expert gardener. What inevitably happens is they get frustrated, and the next planting season, that dirt lays empty and fallow until they sell the home, and a new owner begins the cycle all over again. Starting small takes time, and I understand that it is not flashy enough for most people, but healthy is better than flashy when it comes to growth. Starting small lets you win small and fail small. Small failures hurt less, and small wins inspire you toward bigger goals.

START SMALL WITH CHRIST. LEARN THE EBBS AND FLOWS OF THIS LIFE WITH HIM.

I hope you have been inspired to cultivate a deeper faith in your life. These principles will unlock a vibrancy in your relationship with Christ, but please start small. Try to do only some things simultaneously to avoid burning out. Take one step at a time. Start with cultivating presence and then move on to the other areas. If you try to develop every area at once, you risk falling into the overwhelming approach to faith that this book seeks to alleviate. Start small with Christ. Learn the ebbs and flows of this life with Him. Over time, you will naturally sense the rhythms of grace, the flow of the Spirit, and the seasons of faith. Start small, win big.

BE KIND

Why are we so hard on our own lives? The harshest critic in our own lives is often our own minds. One day, I had a friend over to look at my garden. I had worked for months on this little spot in my yard and felt a general sense of pride at the accomplishment, but something changed when my friend came over. Suddenly, I began apologizing for everything in my garden, pointing out every place where something went wrong and explaining what I was doing about it. It was almost as if I wanted to point out the flaws before they saw them. I noticed halfway through our short tour that I had been increasingly negative about something I loved; all the while, they had been continually impressed, complimenting all the hard work. For some reason, I had spent so much time focusing on the problems that I had not celebrated all the amazing life that had come up from an area that had previously been solid dirt. Insecurity can be a harsh feeling to overcome.

You may feel insecurity rear its ugly head as you begin this journey of cultivation. Be kind to yourself. Be kind to the life you are cultivating. Jesus knows you are not perfect. He knows your shortcomings, yet He graciously longs to deepen your relationship. Don't be too quick to point out the flaws in this garden; just celebrate the wins. Celebrate every place where life is breaking forth, where there was once fallow ground. Rejoice at every place where your faith has gone deeper than you ever imagined, and accept the areas still in progress. Take heart that the Spirit is with you, leading you to a more vibrant life in Christ. Cultivating takes time. Enjoy the process, and be kind to yourself in the journey. The more you cultivate this life in Christ, the more abundant joy will begin to break forth.

www.ingramcontent.com/pod-product-compliance
Lightning Source LLC
Chambersburg PA
CBHW070951180426
43194CB00042B/2272